Becoming
a Catalyst

Insights into the Life of Paul

Gene Getz

MEN of PURPOSE

SERENDIPITY
HOUSE

Becoming a Catalyst: Insights into the Life of Paul
© 2005 Gene Getz

Published by Serendipity House Publishers
Nashville, Tennessee

ISBN: 1-5749-4225-5

Dewey Decimal Classification: 248.842
Subject Headings:
PAUL, APOSTLE \ MEN \ CHRISTIAN LIFE

Unless otherwise indicated, all Scripture quotations are taken from the *Holman Christian Standard Bible®*, Copyright © 1999, 2000, 2002, 2003 by Holman Bible Publishers. Used by permission.

To purchase additional copies of this resource or other studies:
ORDER ONLINE at www.SerendipityHouse.com;
WRITE Serendipity House, 117 10th Avenue North, Nashville, TN 37234
FAX (615) 277-8181
PHONE (800) 525-9563

1-800-525-9563
www.SerendipityHouse.com

Printed in the United States of America
10 09 08 07 06 05 04   1 2 3 4 5 6 7 8 9 10

CONTENTS

Becoming a Catalyst

Insights into the Life of Paul

The term "catalyst" has its origins in the scientific community. A "catalyst" is typically understood as being something that brings about change—usually profound—through a chemical reaction. Change occurs at several junctures in our lives and each profound shift, be it physical, emotional, or intellectual, will usually have a catalyst.

Shortly after I became a Christian, Paul became a catalyst for my life. I will never forget one of my first encounters with this dynamic Jew-turned-Christian. I was a 16-year-old junior in high school, and I had secured a copy of Dr. Kenneth Wuest's commentary on Philippians. With my Bible in one hand and Wuest's explanation in the other, I studied this letter word for word and sentence by sentence.

I was struck by the Greek word *koinonia*, a term Paul used to describe the Philippians' generosity. The "good work" God had begun in their lives (1:6) related directly to their sacrificial spirit in supporting Paul financially. This truth put me on a path in my heart and soul to be a generous Christian. I was a teenager when I learned this lesson from Paul and now, as a senior citizen, I can report that God has never let me down.

My next significant encounter with Paul, the catalyst, occurred two years later. I was 18 and a student at Moody Bible Institute. Since I had been reared in a religious environment that mixed faith and works for salvation, I was not sure that I had eternal life even after I became a Christian.

Early one morning, as I was sitting in my dorm room reading Paul's letter to the Romans, a very pointed question jumped off the page and confronted me: "Who can separate us from the love of Christ?" (Rom. 8:35). Like a cool, calm breeze from heaven, the realization swept over me that I too had been made righteous by faith in Jesus Christ, just as Abraham had been (Rom. 5:1). I have never forgotten that moment of insight. As a catalyst will, it changed my life.

A couple more years went by before I had my third life-changing experience with the Lord through Paul's New Testament letters. I was involved in radio ministry in Billings, Montana. Someone had given me the book *Disciplined by Grace* by John Strombeck, an exposition of Titus 2:11-14.

I had boarded the train in Chicago for a 16-hour trip across the great northwestern states. I opened Strombeck's book and began to read and reflect on what he had to say about Paul's words to Titus. Somewhere between Chicago and Billings, I began to comprehend my freedom in Christ. At the same time, I was deeply challenged never to use this marvelous freedom "as an opportunity for the flesh" (Gal. 5:13). On the contrary, this new spiritual insight motivated me to respond to God's grace with love and holiness.

The lessons that flow from Paul's life and ministry are intensely convicting, motivating, and very practical. Join me in this study and come to know Paul as a catalyst. Then you, too, can respond to his exhortation to the Corinthians: "Be imitators of me, as I also am of Christ" (1 Cor. 11:1).

How to use this book

While this Bible study may be used individually, it is designed to be used within the context of small groups. Each group meeting should include all elements of the following "three-part agenda."

Icebreaker: Fun, history-giving questions are designed to warm up the group and build understanding between group members. You may choose to use all of the Icebreaker questions, especially if there is a new group member who will need help in feeling comfortable with the group.

One of the purposes of this book is to begin and to then solidify a group. Therefore, getting to know one another and bonding together are essential to the success of this effort. The Icebreaker segment in each group session is designed to help you become better acquainted, greatly enhancing your group experience.

Bible Study: The heart of each meeting is your examination together of the Bible and the key "Principles to Live By" that are drawn from it. This section emphasizes understanding what the Bible says and applying its truth to real life. The questions are open discovery questions that lead to further inquiry. Reference notes are provided to give everyone a level playing field and provide deeper insights into the biblical story. The questions for each session build on one another. There are always Going Deeper questions provided. Be mindful to always leave time for the last of the Questions for Interaction. You may elect to use the optional Going Deeper questions to lead you in applying what the group has learned. This segment also satisfies the desire for more challenging questions in groups that have been together for a while.

To help your men connect as a group, it is important for everyone to participate in the Bible study. There are no right or wrong answers to the questions. Participants should strive to make all of the other group members feel comfortable during the Bible study time. Because we all have differing levels of biblical knowledge, it is essential that we understand and appreciate the personal context from which each one of us responds. We don't have to know much about theology and history to bring our own perspectives to bear on the truths contained in the Scriptures. It is vital that you keep encouraging all group members to share what they are observing as you work through these important Bible passages.

Caring Time: All study should lead us to action. Each session ends with prayer and direction in caring for the needs of individual group members. You can choose between the various questions provided, or use them all.

Small groups help the larger body of Christ in many ways: caring for individuals, holding one another up in prayer, providing emotional support, and bringing new men into the church family. Each week it is important to remember to pray for those whom God would bring to your group.

HOW TO GET THE MOST OUT OF THIS BOOK

Begin by reviewing the following ground rules and talk about the importance of "sharing your story" (see below).

GROUND RULES

- **Priority:** While you are in the group, give the group meeting priority.

- **Participation:** Everyone participates and no one dominates.

- **Respect:** Everyone is given the right to his own opinion and all questions are encouraged ... and respected.

- **Confidentiality:** Anything that is said in the meeting is never repeated outside the meeting.

- **Empty Chair:** The group stays open to inviting new men to every meeting. Keeping an empty chair in your circle symbolizes those men you need to invite.

- **Support:** Permission is given to call upon each other in time of need—even in the middle of the night.

- **Advice Giving:** Unsolicited advice is not allowed.

- **Mission:** We agree to do everything in our power to work toward starting a new group—a vital part of our mission.

SHARING YOUR STORY

These sessions are designed to encourage group members to share a little of their personal lives each time the group meets. Through a number of special techniques, each member is encouraged to move from low risk, less personal sharing to higher risk responses. This helps develop authentic community and facilitates care-giving within your group.

It is only when group members begin to share their own stories that the group bonds at levels deep enough for life-change to take place.

SINCERELY WRONG

It is unlikely we will ever meet someone whose sincerity prior to conversion is greater than Paul's. Neither will we meet anyone who is so woefully mistaken and misguided as he. Many people make bad decisions and choices due to wrong motives. They know there is something bad about what they are doing. Not so with Paul. He could say, "It was out of ignorance that I had acted in unbelief" (1 Tim. 1:13). With all his heart, he thought he was right. One of the greatest lessons we can learn from Paul's life is that it is possible to be very earnest and fervent in our beliefs and behavior and still be completely wrong.

ICEBREAKER

Probably every man in this group has come to question and rethink some aspect of the religious, political, or racial values handed down to him by his family heritage. Sometimes, such reevaluation forms part of the reason for teenage rebellion. It can also happen as a result of higher education. Other times, this may occur as the result of some crisis later in life.

1. When you were a boy, which of these characters were you most disappointed to discover wasn't real? How did you make this unhappy discovery?
   a. Santa Claus
   b. The Easter Bunny
   c. The Tooth Fairy
   d. Spiderman
   e. Other _____

2. When you were a teenager, what family belief, tradition, or practice embarrassed you most?

3. As an adult, what belief that you learned from your family and once held zealously have you abandoned?

LESSON 1

Paul—or Saul of Tarsus, as he was known in Jewish circles—first appears in the pages of Scripture guarding the clothes of those who stoned Stephen in Acts 7:58. Through the course of Acts and the letters of Paul, we can pick up various hints about Paul's earlier life and the events that led up to his dramatic encounter with the risen Lord Jesus Christ on the road to Damascus.

A Sincere Jewish Heritage

[I was] [5] circumcised the eighth day; of the nation of Israel, of the tribe of Benjamin, a Hebrew born of Hebrews; as to the law, a Pharisee; [6] as to zeal, persecuting the church; as to the righteousness that is in the law, blameless.

Philippians 3:5-6

A Prestigious Roman Citizenship

[25] As they stretched him out for the lash, Paul said to the centurion standing by, "Is it legal for you to scourge a man who is a Roman citizen and is uncondemned?"

[26] When the centurion heard this, he went and reported to the commander, saying, "What are you going to do? For this man is a Roman citizen."

[27] The commander came and said to him, "Tell me—are you a Roman citizen?"

"Yes," he said.

[28] The commander replied, "I bought this citizenship for a large amount of money."

"But I myself was born a citizen," Paul said.

Acts 22:25-28

A Persecutor of the Church

[3] He continued, "I am a Jewish man, born in Tarsus of Cilicia, but brought up in this city at the feet of Gamaliel, and educated according to the strict view of our patriarchal law. Being zealous for God, just as all of you are today, [4] I persecuted this Way to the death, binding and putting both men and women in jail, [5] as both the high priest and the whole council of elders can testify about me. Having received letters from them to the brothers, I was traveling to Damascus to bring those who were prisoners there to be punished in Jerusalem.

Acts 22:3-5

[8] Stephen, full of grace and power, was performing great wonders and signs among the people. [9] Then some from what is called the Freedmen's

Synagogue, composed of both Cyrenians and Alexandrians, and some from Cilicia and Asia, came forward and disputed with Stephen. ... [12] They stirred up the people, the elders, and the scribes; so they came up, dragged him off, and took him to the Sanhedrin. ...

[58] They threw him out of the city and began to stone him. And the witnesses laid their robes at the feet of a young man named Saul. [59] They were stoning Stephen as he called out: "Lord Jesus, receive my spirit!" [60] Then he knelt down and cried out with a loud voice, "Lord, do not charge them with this sin!" And saying this, he fell asleep.
[1] Saul agreed with putting him to death. On that day a severe persecution broke out against the church in Jerusalem, and all except the apostles were scattered throughout the land of Judea and Samaria. [2] But devout men buried Stephen and mourned deeply over him. [3] Saul, however, was ravaging the church, and he would enter house after house, drag off men and women, and put them in prison.

Acts 6:8-9,12; 7:58–8:3

[9] In fact, I myself supposed it was necessary to do many things in opposition to the name of Jesus the Nazarene. [10] This I actually did in Jerusalem, and I locked up many of the saints in prison, since I had received authority for that from the chief priests. When they were put to death, I cast my vote against them. [11] In all the synagogues I often tried to make them blaspheme by punishing them. Being greatly enraged at them, I even pursued them to foreign cities.

Acts 26:9-11

A Gracious Forgiveness

[I was] [13] one who was formerly a blasphemer, a persecutor, and an arrogant man. Since it was out of ignorance that I had acted in unbelief, I received mercy.

1 Timothy 1:13

PRINCIPLES TO LIVE BY

Most of us have grown up with some ideas about religion that we need to square with the Word of God. Maybe our church was exclusive and critical of other faith traditions. Perhaps we grew up in circles that believed all religions are paths to the "one God known by many names." On the other hand, we may have been taught to scoff at belief in God. Whatever your family's spiritual belief system, you had the choice of embracing it eagerly, warmly, or coldly. Paul's example offers warnings to those of us who tend to go overboard in our religious zeal.

WE CAN BE INTENSELY ZEALOUS ABOUT OUR RELIGIOUS OR PHILO-
SOPHICAL BELIEFS AND STILL BE SINCERELY WRONG.

Paul grew up in Tarsus, a city with about 500,000 inhabitants that was
also the capital of Cilicia, a Roman province in eastern Asia Minor. Tarsus
was a "free city" within the Roman Empire so its citizens enjoyed imperial
citizenship. In addition to the rights and priviledges associated with Roman citizenship, Paul received rigorous instruction in the local synagogue
along with other young men from Jewish families and learned the trade of
tentmaking.

Around the age of 13, Paul went to Jerusalem to receive intensive rab-
binic training from Gamaliel, the leader of the Hillel school of Pharisaic
thought. He would have finished this training before his twentieth birth-
day and then no doubt ministered in a synagogue in Tarsus. When we first
meet Paul, he is in Jerusalem and is probably about 35 years old.

Paul was terribly frustrated with the numerical growth of those proclaiming to be disciples of Jesus of Nazareth. His anger grew as more and
more fellow Jews defected from the teachings of Moses. Consequently,
he wholeheartedly approved the execution of Stephen and launched an
all-out war against Jews who declared their allegiance to Jesus. He began
"ravaging the church." He would "enter house after house" in order to
"drag off men and women, and put them in prison" (Acts 8:3). Soon he
took his campaign to other cities of Judea. Eventually he struck as far
afield as Damascus, until the Lord stopped him in his tracks.

Though most of us who grow up in a free society do not act on our
religious convictions to the same degree as Paul, we can become very opin-
ionated about our beliefs. This often happens when we have been taught a
certain belief system from childhood.

Remember that Paul's attacks were not against the pagans in the
Roman Empire, but against his fellow Jews who had departed from what
he believed was the straight and narrow path. Similarly, religious leaders
today can become very hostile toward people who leave their folds. Sadly,
many believe they are right, but like Paul, they are sincerely wrong.

WE CAN BE EXTREMELY ARTICULATE OR WISE AND STILL BE SIN-
CERELY WRONG.

Paul was a gifted and highly educated product of two cultures. He learned
theology from the synagogue schools of his boyhood and from the rigor-

ous curriculum of Gamaliel. He was a Pharisee of the Pharisees, but he also knew the literature and philosophy of paganism. He could refer to relatively obscure authors to establish common ground with the intelligentsia of Athens. However, he was still spiritually blind until he encountered Jesus Christ on the Damascus Road.

In many cases, an extensive education can actually contribute to having a closed mind regarding God's revelation. The reason is simple. The more we learn, the more we can be in bondage to our own egos. Paul recognized this after his conversion when he wrote to the Corinthians, "Knowledge inflates with pride, but love builds up" (1 Cor. 8:1).

Does this mean that all education is evil, as some religious groups believe? The answer is a decided no. We need more scholars who are Christians. But on the other hand, Paul warned against the negative influence of "human wisdom" (1 Cor. 2:12-13). James echoed this same concern when he wrote about "wisdom" that "is earthly, sensual" and even "demonic" (Jas. 3:15).

Paul also had some straightforward and enlightening words for non-Christians. He remembered well his own unconverted state of mind. "The natural man does not welcome what comes from God's Spirit, because it is foolishness to him; he is not able to know it since it is evaluated spiritually" (1 Cor. 2:14).

QUESTIONS FOR INTERACTION

1. In our age of tolerance, people sometimes say, "It doesn't matter what you believe as long as you're sincere." What's right about that statement? What's wrong with it?

2. Why did Paul have reason to be confident of his education and the opinions he held (Acts 22:3; Phil. 3:5-6)?

3. What did Paul think he was doing when he persecuted the church of Jesus Christ (Acts 22:3b-4; 26:9; Phil. 3:6)?

4. What measures did Paul employ to oppose the church (Acts 22:4-5; 26:10-11)?

5. In reality, what was going on in the spiritual realm when Paul engaged in persecution?

6. How was Satan able to convince Paul that he was serving God, when in fact he was attacking the people of God?

7. How does Satan convince Christians today that they are doing the right thing by attacking fellow Christians who disagree with them?

8. What are some of the consequences of being sincerely wrong? What consequences have you faced because of being sincerely wrong?

GOING DEEPER

9. How would you go about talking with a fellow believer whom you're convinced is sincerely wrong about an important belief?

10. How would you want to be approached by someone who felt you were sincerely wrong about a belief or behavior?

11. What Scriptures should we keep in mind when approaching a brother in Christ who is sincerely wrong in belief or behavior?

12. What is good about being reluctant to confront a brother we think may be sincerely wrong? What is bad about such reluctance?

CARING TIME

It can be overwhelming to study the life of a person like Paul. Here was a high-energy man on a fast track to prominence, prestige, and power. He had the right credentials, the right connections, and all kinds of confidence. Then when things blew up in Judaism, he just took off and made a big noise in the Christian community. Can we really relate to such a larger-than-life character? Even when he was wrong, he was so sincere about it that it puts most of us to shame.

As we study Paul's life and ministry, let us pray for one another with zeal and sincerity. Let us learn from Paul how to follow God's truth and purpose for our lives.

1. Which of these statements best compares you and Paul?
   a. I'm a high-energy, high-drive guy bent on getting tasks done, very much like Paul.
   b. I'm more relationship-oriented than task-oriented, but I'm a go-getter.
   c. I'm much more laid-back than Paul, but I like to be around heavy hitters.
   d. I want a quiet life. Guys like Paul intimidate me. I avoid them.

2. What are some of the strengths and weaknesses associated with what you revealed about yourself in question 1?

3. How do you tend to protect yourself when you feel someone is being critical of you? How will you react in this group if someone should confront you about your beliefs or behaviors?

NEXT WEEK

Next week we will look at how God intervened in the life of Paul and brought him to saving faith in Jesus Christ. At the very height of his career as a persecutor of Christians, Paul abruptly changed sides and joined those he had violently opposed. Like so much about this man, Paul's conversion was such an overwhelming, supernatural experience that it dramatically illustrates important truths about our own conversions.

SCRIPTURE NOTES

ACTS 6:8-9,12; 7:58–8:3; 22:3-5,25-28; 26:9-11

6:9 the Feedmen's Synagogue. The Freedmen were former Roman slaves (or their descendants) released by their masters and granted Roman citizenship.

7:58 John 18:31 indicates the Sanhedrin did not have the legal right to carry out capital punishment, so this may be an act of mob violence. However, Acts 26:10 indicates that perhaps by this time Pilate's ability to control the Sanhedrin had drastically weakened and it indeed took capital cases into its own hands. **Saul.** Jewish men commonly had a biblical name given at birth and a Gentile name they adopted for use outside the Jewish community. Saul was named for the first king of Israel, the most famous Old Testament Benjamite. Among the Gentile churches, he would be known as Paul (Latin: Paulus).

8:1-3 Some biblical scholars don't think Acts 26:10 is sufficient evidence that Saul belonged to the Sanhedrin, but he quickly became the leading figure in a violent persecution of the church.

8:3 ravaging. This word is used to describe how a beast rips the flesh off its victim. Saul's persecution led to other Christians being condemned to death as well (9:1-2).

22:3 Jewish man ... brought up in this city. Although a citizen of Tarsus by virtue of his birth, Paul had spent most of his teen years in Jerusalem. Acts 23:16 implies that Paul's sister and her family lived there. **Gamaliel.** Gamaliel was a highly respected Pharisee, head of the Hillel wing of this sect. To have received an education from this man was to have had access to the best possible Jewish education (5:34). *our patriarchal law*. Paul emphasized that he too had a lifelong knowledge of and respect for the Law.

22:4 this Way. Unique to the Book of Acts as a name for Christianity (19:9,23; 24:14,22).

22:25 Flogging was a severe punishment since leather thongs weighted with pieces of bone, metal, or rocks were used as the whip. Roman citizens were protected from punishment without trial and were sheltered from this particular form of punishment no matter what; therefore, Paul once again brought up the matter of his Roman citizenship (16:37).

22:28 I bought this citizenship for a large amount of money. Citizenship was not supposedly a matter of money, but of birthright or notable service. However, bribes and other means of influence were also ways of gaining the privilege. *I myself was born a citizen*. Paul's response turns the tables on the commander. His citizenship was not a matter of bribery at all, but of natural right.

PHILIPPIANS 3:5-6

3:5 eighth day. It was on the eighth day after birth that a Jewish baby boy (as opposed to an adult proselyte) was circumcised. Paul was a true Jew from the time of his birth. *the tribe of Benjamin*. The members of the tribe of Benjamin constituted an elite group within Israel. *a Pharisee*. He was one of the spiritual elite in Israel.

3:6 as to zeal, persecuting the church. Zeal was a highly prized virtue among the Jews. Paul had demonstrated his zeal for the Law by ferreting out Christians and bringing them to trial (Acts 22:4-5; 26:9-11). *blameless*. To the best of his ability, Paul tried to observe the whole Law. Taken together, all these attributes mean that Paul was in every way the match of his Jewish opponents in Philippi who belittled his qualifications to speak authoritatively about spiritual issues. He had lived at the very pinnacle of Judaism.

1 TIMOTHY 1:13

1:13 blasphemer. Paul had denied Christ and tried to force others to do the same (Acts 26:11). *a persecutor, and an arrogant man*. He had actively opposed the church—searching out Christians, arresting them, throwing them in prison, even voting for their deaths. *it was out of ignorance that I had acted in unbelief*. Paul is not saying that he had received mercy because he was without guilt. All he is saying is that he acted "unintentionally" instead of "defiantly," using a common Old Testament distinction (Num. 15:22-31; Luke 23:34).

INSIDE AND OUT

LAST WEEK

In the first lesson of this study, we examined the physical and spiritual heritage of the Apostle Paul. We saw how his zeal for "righteousness" led him to persecute the church of Jesus Christ. Paul's example cautions us against allowing unexamined religious traditions to become the basis for unwarranted criticism of other Christians.

ICEBREAKER

Paul became so passionate about opposing Christianity that he took his crusade show on the road. He made it his career to bust Christians for their beliefs and to force them to deny their new faith. He changed his whole way of life to pursue this passion.

1. What is the longest trip you ever made? How did your body react to the travel and all the changes involved in adapting to a new place?

2. Which of these statements best describes how you react to a big, high-stress project?
     a. I'm Mr. Bring-It-On-I-Love-This.
     b. I'm Mr. I-Can-Do-It-If-I-Need-To.
     c. I'm Mr. Sweaty-Palms-Until-It's-Over.
     d. I'm Mr. Can't-Sleep-Can't-Eat-All-Week-For-Worry.
     e. Other _____.

What is something you're so passionate about that you talk about it all the time? How do others react to your grand passion?

BIBLICAL FOUNDATION

The term *intervention* refers to the process of confronting people we love about destructive patterns of life that need to change before they cause irreparable damage. Paul's encounter with Christ on the Damascus Road stands out as one of the most dramatic and significant interventions ever recorded. It was a supernatural intervention by God the Father, Jesus Christ the Son, and the blessed Holy Spirit. Speaking directly from heaven, Jesus served as the divine spokesman for the Holy Trinity. This supernatural intervention led to Paul's supernatural conversion. This dramatic intervention culminated with dramatic transformation—inside and out. Although Paul is still referred to as Saul throughout these passages. Luke begins referring to him by his Gentile name, Paul, in Acts 13:9 as he and Barnabas launch their first missionary venture targeting non-Jews, as well as Jews, on the island of Cyprus.

Paul Sees the Light

[1] Saul agreed with putting [Stephen] to death.
On that day a severe persecution broke out against the church in Jerusalem, and all except the apostles were scattered throughout the land of Judea and Samaria. [2] But devout men buried Stephen and mourned deeply over him. [3] Saul, however, was ravaging the church, and he would enter house after house, drag off men and women, and put them in prison.

Acts 8:1-3

[9] In fact, I myself supposed it was necessary to do many things in opposition to the name of Jesus the Nazarene. [10] This I actually did in Jerusalem, and I locked up many of the saints in prison, since I had received authority for that from the chief priests. When they were put to death, I cast my vote against them. [11] In all the synagogues I often tried to make them blaspheme by punishing them. Being greatly enraged at them, I even pursued them to foreign cities.
[12] "Under these circumstances I was traveling to Damascus with authority and a commission from the chief priests."

Acts 26:9-12

[3] As he traveled and was nearing Damascus, a light from heaven suddenly flashed around him. 4 Falling to the ground, he heard a voice saying to him, "Saul, Saul, why are you persecuting Me?"
[5] "Who are You, Lord?" he said.
"I am Jesus, whom you are persecuting," He replied. [6] "But get up and go into the city, and you will be told what you must do."
[7] The men who were traveling with him stood speechless, hearing the sound but seeing no one. [8] Then Saul got up from the ground, and though his eyes were open, he could see nothing. So they took him by the hand and led him into Damascus. [9] He was unable to see for three days, and did not eat or drink.
[10] Now in Damascus there was a disciple named Ananias. And the Lord said to him in a vision, "Ananias!"
"Here I am, Lord!" he said.
[11] "Get up and go to the street called Straight," the Lord said to him, "to

the house of Judas, and ask for a man from Tarsus named Saul, since he is praying there. [12] In a vision he has seen a man named Ananias coming in and placing his hands on him so he may regain his sight." ...

[17] So Ananias left and entered the house. Then he placed his hands on him and said, "Brother Saul, the Lord Jesus, who appeared to you on the road you were traveling, has sent me so you may regain your sight and be filled with the Holy Spirit."

[18] At once something like scales fell from his eyes, and he regained his sight. Then he got up and was baptized. [19] And after taking some food, he regained his strength.

Acts 9:3-12,17-19

PRINCIPLES TO LIVE BY

Paul's encounter with the Lord Jesus was extremely dramatic. Most likely, our conversion experiences differ strikingly in external details from his. However, internally, we all meet Jesus quite similarly. Once we see beyond Paul's physical experience and analyze his spiritual experience, we can learn a great deal that applies to our own lives and the lives of those around us.

PRINCIPLE 1

GOD'S DESIRE IS THAT ALL PEOPLE ADMIT THEIR SINS, ACCEPT THAT THEY FALL SHORT OF WHO THEY HAVE BEEN CREATED TO BE, AND INVITE THE LORD JESUS CHRIST TO BE THEIR SAVIOR.

Following his approval of Stephen's death, Paul immediately turned up the heat in his determination to stamp out Christianity. What began as a rather spontaneous act of hatred quickly evolved into a cruel, organized effort.

Paul wasn't satisfied to restrict his vicious attacks on Christians to Jerusalem. Years later he told King Agrippa, "Being greatly enraged at them, I even pursued them to foreign cities" (Acts 26:11b). The last of those "foreign cities" proved to be Damascus.

As Paul traveled the road to Damascus, the Lord Jesus confronted him under the guise of a bright light and a voice like thunder. At this point Paul, this persecutor of Christians, acknowledged Jesus Christ as Lord. His conversion occurred during those moments between the time he fell to the ground, heard Jesus' voice (Acts 9:4), and then cried out, "Who are You, Lord?" (v. 5).

On Paul's second missionary journey, the Philippian jailer asked him, "What must I do to be saved?" (Acts 16:30). Paul replied, "Believe on the Lord Jesus, and you will be saved" (v. 31). That is what happened to Paul on the road to Damascus. That is what God wants for every human born into this world. As the Apostle Peter reminds us: "The Lord ... is patient with you, not wanting any to perish, but all to come to repentance" (2 Pet. 3:9).

PRINCIPLE 2

GOD'S DESIRE IS THAT ALL BELIEVERS BE BAPTIZED AS AN EXTERNAL EXPRESSION OF A NEW LIFE IN JESUS.

God directed a Jewish believer named Ananias, who lived in Damascus, to go to the house where Paul waited to be delivered from the blindness that resulted from the bright light that was the presence of Jesus. Ananias laid his hands on Paul and his eyes were healed.

For three days, Paul had neither eaten nor drunk anything as a result of the trauma of meeting Jesus (Acts 9:9). However, as soon as he could see again, he insisted on being baptized (v. 18). Only then would he take something to eat and drink (v. 19). Clearly, Paul was eager to identify quickly and decisively with the followers of Jesus, just as the Lord had commanded (Matt. 28:19-20).

God designed water baptism to be an outward sign of an inward reality. The inward reality is that by faith we die with Christ, are buried with Him, and are raised to a new life (Rom. 6:4). The outward symbol simply illustrates what has already happened in our hearts. Going into the water symbolizes death. Rising from the water symbolizes our resurrection and new life that results from our faith in the Lord Jesus Christ.

PRINCIPLE 3

GOD'S DESIRE IS THAT WE RESPOND QUICKLY TO THE HOLY SPIRIT'S CONVICTION.

Luke includes three accounts of Paul's conversion in the Book of Acts. The first is Luke's narration of the event (Acts 9:1-12). The second occurs in Paul's defense to the mob at the temple (22:6-21). The third can be found in Paul's testimony before Governor Felix and King Agrippa (26:12-18).

In Paul's testimony before Felix and Agrippa he recalls the words of Jesus, "It is hard for you to kick against the goads" (26:14). Goads were sharp sticks, sometimes metal-tipped, used by herdsmen to steer livestock by means of quick jabs from the side or the rear. A stubborn animal determined not to go where the herdsman directed it might kick up its hind legs to deflect the goads. Paul's intent in using these particular words was twofold: (1) there is pain associated with kicking against the goads and (2) taking this action is, frankly, a waste of time.

Even while Paul had persecuted the church, the Holy Spirit had been convicting his heart of the truth about Jesus. Paul had heard Stephen preach (7:2-53). He had seen Stephen's face transformed before he died (6:15). He had heard Stephen declare that he saw Jesus (7:56). He heard Stephen ask the Lord to forgive his executioners (v. 60). The Holy Spirit had been pricking Paul's conscience with these memories and those of others who had faced up to persecution in the power of the Lord.

In moments of aloneness, Stephen's final words had rung in Paul's ears, but he had repeatedly ignored the prodding of the Holy Spirit. Because Paul was acting in ignorance (1 Tim. 1:13), God had mercy on him. Jesus intervened in Paul's life and, as a result, Paul yielded to the conviction of the Holy Spirit. Today the Spirit continues to appeal to sinners, convicting them of "sin, righteousness, and judgment" (John 16:8). The appeal still rings out: "Everyone who believes in Him will not perish but have eternal life" (3:16).

QUESTIONS FOR INTERACTION

1. How would you rate the chances of your conversion story being made into a movie-of-the-week?
    a. I'm not sure I have a conversion story.
    b. Two thumbs down. It's a kid's story.
    c. One thumb up, one down. Too much like all the others.
    d. Two thumbs way up. Lots of juicy stuff.

2. What are the benefits of hearing the stories of other people's conversions?

3. What was Paul's strategy for stopping the spread of Christianity? What punishments awaited those who fell into Paul's clutches (Acts 8:3; 26:9-11)?

4. Why do you think it was necessary for Jesus to confront Paul so dramatically (9:3-9)? Why not change him gradually?

5. How might a psychiatrist try to explain Paul's conversion experience? A doctor? An astrologer?

6. Why would Jesus want Paul to wait for Ananias, instead of healing his eyes personally right then (9:10-12,17-19)?

7. What do you suppose Paul thought about during the three days he waited for Ananias?

8. How do you tend to react to stories of dramatic conversions? Why do you react this way?
   a. Wow! Isn't God great?
   b. Wow! That must have been exciting for that person.
   c. Wow! I wish that had been me.
   d. Hmmm. I wonder if he's embellishing a little?
   e. Hmmm. I wonder what he's selling?
   f. Ho-hum. Another one.
   g. Other _____.

9. Have the changes in your life since conversion been dramatic, gradual, or a mix of both? Tell about some of them.

GOING DEEPER

10. In what ways did you resist the message of salvation and experience the convicting ministry of the Holy Spirit?

11. Why did the early Christians place so much emphasis on baptism? What does the memory of your baptism mean to you?

12. Who played the role of Ananias and helped you get your feet on the ground as a new Christian?

CARING TIME

Early in this small-group study, it is good to consider those in our circles of acquaintances who need to know Christ as Savior. As we grow in our discipleship, we must never lose sight of the need to share our faith with unbelievers. This lesson on Paul's saving encounter with Christ gives us a good opportunity to remember our evangelistic responsibility.

1. Among your family, friends, and coworkers, for whom should you pray with regard to salvation? Who might you invite to this men's group?

2. Narrow your list to one primary person on whom you will focus your prayers and sharing throughout the course of this study about Paul.

3. Close by praying for the man to your right that God would bless his witness to the person he named.

NEXT WEEK

Next week we will look at the changes the Lord began to make in Paul's life after he came to saving faith in Jesus Christ. Luke gives us a very condensed account of the next few years of Paul's life. In his epistles, Paul fills in enough of the gaps that we can piece together the process the Holy Spirit took Paul through in order to transform his understanding of what God was up to in the world. Like most things he did, Paul fervently learned about the gospel of Christ with all his heart, mind, and strength.

SCRIPTURE NOTES

ACTS 8:1-3; 9:3-12,17-19; 26:9-12

8:1-3 Some biblical scholars don't think Acts 26:10 is sufficient evidence that Saul belonged to the Sanhedrin, but he quickly became the leading figure in a violent persecution of the church.

8:3 ravaging. This word is used to describe how a beast rips the flesh off its victim. Saul's persecution led to other Christians being condemned to death as well (9:1-2).

9:3 a light from heaven suddenly flashed around him. This description is often used of lightning, indicating the brilliance of the light (26:13). Light (glory) is commonly connected with divine appearance (Luke 9:29; Rev. 1:14-16).

9:10 Apart from Paul's comments in 22:12, nothing is known of Ananias.

9:11 to the street called Straight ... to the house of Judas. The "street called Straight" where Saul's host lived, is still one of the chief thoroughfares of Damascus. The house of Judas is traditionally located near its western end. Nothing is known of Judas.

9:17 Brother Saul. Without further question, Ananias affirmed Saul as part of the family through the grace of Jesus. After Ananias laid hands on him, Saul's sight was restored, he was baptized (presumably by Ananias), and he was filled by with the Holy Spirit.

THE METAMORPHOSIS

LAST WEEK

Last week we studied the dramatic conversion of Paul. We saw that the external details of his encounter with Christ may have differed markedly from ours, but the internal, spiritual issues were the same. We were reminded that the Lord desires all of us to come to know Him as Savior. He seeks us all, whether great in the eyes of the world or quite ordinary. He wants us to witness to our faith through baptism.

ICEBREAKER

Change is part of modern life. Jobs don't last. People often move. Fads and fashions come and go before most of us notice. We get used to rapid change—sort of. However, a lot of us aren't nearly as fond of change as the futurists tell us we're supposed to be.

1. Which of these major changes did you experience as a boy? How did it (they) affect you?
   a. Moving/Changing schools
   b. Divorce of parents
   c. Serious injury or illness
   d. Death of parent, relative, or good friend
   e. Other _____

2. Which of these nasty tricks did puberty pull on you? Which had the greatest impact on you?
   a. "Pizza-face" acne
   b. Weird voice changes
   c. Over-the-top sexual urges
   d. Unpredictable emotional reactions
   e. A high velocity growth spurt
   f. Other _____

3. What do you like best about living in a world of rapid change? What do you like least?

The biblical account of how various people reacted to Paul's conversion is brief, but it is clear that everyone was startled and unsure as to how to react to the news of his change of heart. It certainly was stirring and even electrifying for those Jews who had already accepted Jesus as the Christ or Messiah. On the other hand, Paul's transformation was definitely unnerving and threatening for those unbelieving Jews who witnessed what happened.

In the following Scriptures, Galatians 1:11-17 is placed between Acts 9:21 and 22. It seems best to locate Paul's Arabian pilgrimage between these two aspects of his ministry in Damascus.

Renewing Paul's Mind

[19] And after taking some food, he regained his strength. Saul was with the disciples in Damascus for some days. [20] Immediately he began proclaiming Jesus in the synagogues: "He is the Son of God." [21] But all who heard him were astounded and said, "Isn't this the man who, in Jerusalem, was destroying those who called on this name, and then came here for the purpose of taking them as prisoners to the chief priests?"

Acts 9:19-21

[11] Now I want you to know, brothers, that the gospel preached by me is not based on a human point of view. [12] For I did not receive it from a human source and I was not taught it, but it came by a revelation from Jesus Christ.
[13] For you have heard about my former way of life in Judaism: I persecuted God's church to an extreme degree and tried to destroy it; [14] and I advanced in Judaism beyond many contemporaries among my people, because I was extremely zealous for the traditions of my ancestors. [15] But when God, who from my mother's womb set me apart and called me by His grace, was pleased [16] to reveal His Son in me, so that I could preach Him among the Gentiles, I did not immediately consult with anyone. [17] I did not go up to Jerusalem to those who had become apostles before me; instead I went to Arabia and came back to Damascus.

Galatians 1:11-17

[22] But Saul grew more capable, and kept confounding the Jews who lived in Damascus by proving that this One is the Messiah.

Acts 9:22

[9] For I am the least of the apostles, unworthy to be called an apostle, because I persecuted the church of God. [10] But by God's grace I am what

I am, and His grace toward me was not ineffective. However, I worked more than any of them, yet not I, but God's grace that was in me.

1 Corinthians 15:9-10

PRINCIPLES TO LIVE BY

Though few, if any, of us will ever be able to identify with the intense drama and miraculous aspects of Paul's calling and life changes, we can identify with the supernatural aspects of new birth and the transforming power of Jesus Christ. Conversion is a glorious moment with eternal ramifications, but the experiences that make our character and mark the milestones of a well-lived life come afterward as we cooperate with the Spirit of God in the grand process of sanctification.

PRINCIPLE 1

GOD SEEKS TO TRANSFORM EVERY BELIEVER INTO A GREATER AND GREATER LIKENESS WITH JESUS.

Paul's personal encounter with Jesus was indeed life changing, not only in terms of his eternal destiny but also in terms of his day-to-day behavior. Even so, it must be noted that Paul wasn't himself seeking such a change. Rather, it was God seeking Paul's transformation. After Jesus appeared to him, Paul experienced blindness for three days. Whatever the Lord had in mind for Paul, no one can deny that those three days without sight set the stage for one of the most remarkable and momentous "new-life" transformations of all time.

During the few days he stayed in Damascus, Paul immediately "began proclaiming Jesus in the synagogues" (Acts 9:20). It soon became clear to Paul that he was not ready to engage in debate with the learned rabbis, so he withdrew for two or three years of intensive study and reflection in Arabia (Gal. 1:17). In the solitude of his Arabian retreat, Paul studied and reflected on the Old Testament Scriptures about the Messiah. He also received revelations from God about the nature of the gospel and the church (vv. 11-12,16-17; Eph. 3:2-3).

When Paul returned to Damascus from Arabia (Gal. 1:17) he could now do more than proclaim Christ. He proved from the Old Testament Scriptures that Jesus was the Messiah (Acts 9:22). He was beginning to function as an apostle. Christ had commissioned Paul at the time of his conversion (26:16-18). He had studied in solitude, where he received revelations that confirmed his ministry as an apostle. Now it began in earnest. In his letters, Paul instructs us all to cooperate with the Holy Spirit as He engages in the process of transforming us into the likeness of the character of Christ. We "are being renewed in the spirit of [our] minds." We "took off" our "old man" and "put on the new man, the one created according to God's likeness in righteousness and purity of the truth" (Eph. 4:22-24). This transformation should be evident in every true Christian's life. However, there will be a great deal of diversity in our various experiences.

PRINCIPLE 2

GOD RENEWS OUR MINDS AND TRANSFORMS OUR CHARACTERS THROUGH PROCESSES AND MEASURES UNIQUE TO EACH OF US AS INDIVIDUALS.

The process of transformation went on throughout Paul's lifetime, and it does in our lives as well. Some changes occur quickly. Some take a long time. We should not pattern our transformation after that of Paul in the Bible or of other Christians today. The Holy Spirit intends on conforming us to the image of Christ. He has a plan tailored to our individual needs. What God expects of us is that we renew our minds by immersing ourselves in the Scriptures (Rom. 12:2), as Paul did in Arabia. If we do not renew our minds, we will grieve the Holy Spirit as we resist His sanctifying work in our lives (Eph. 4:30).

Some people have, like Timothy, "known the sacred Scriptures" from the time they could hear and understand (2 Tim. 3:15). In a way, Paul had been like this in Judaism. From childhood, he had devoted himself to keeping the Law of Moses. Unlike Timothy, Paul did not easily understand that Jesus was the Messiah promised by the Old Testament prophets. He angrily rejected the Christian gospel and tried to destroy the Jews who became disciples of Christ. It took a crisis on the Damascus Road to cause Paul to recognize Jesus as the Messiah.

QUESTIONS FOR INTERACTION

1. What is the most significant transformation the Lord has worked in your life since you became a Christian?

2. Which aspect of your character would you like to see the Holy Spirit transform next?

3. Do the Scriptures provided in Biblical Foundations suggest Paul to be more of a man of action or a man of contemplation? Why?

4. Why do you suppose Paul felt he should immediately preach about Jesus? Why would his message be "He is the Son of God" (Acts 9:20)?

5. How did Paul's ministry in Damascus change from before his extended "study leave" in Arabia (v. 21) to after it (v. 22)?

6. Why was it important that Christ reveal Himself directly to Paul instead of allowing him to be taught by the original apostles (Gal. 1:11-17)?

7. What changed about Paul immediately upon conversion? What things about him stayed the same? What things changed over time?

8. How could Paul claim it was the grace of God, rather than his own will-power, that made him the hardest-working apostle (1 Cor. 15:9-10)?

9. How did you express your enthusiasm about Christ immediately after your conversion (or a subsequent life-altering encounter with the Lord)?

GOING DEEPER

10. How effectively have you allowed the Scriptures to reprogram the way you think about life? What do you need to do to take the renewal of your mind to the next level?

11. We can grieve the Holy Spirit (Eph. 4:30) and stifle His transforming work (1 Thess. 5:19). How might we do this intentionally? How might we do it unintentionally?

12. How can different Christians, equally committed to being transformed by the Word of God and the Holy Spirit, turn out with markedly different ideas and patterns of behavior?

CARING TIME

This lesson gives us an opportunity as men to renew our commitment to cooperating with God's Holy Spirit as He works to transform our lives and character into the image of Jesus Christ. We need to be committed to helping one another put off "the old man" and put on "the new man" (Eph. 4:22-24). This kind of cooperation with the Spirit is an invaluable way "iron sharpens iron" in a group of men (Prov. 27:17).

1. Discuss among yourselves what kind of Scripture reading and/or memorization program each of you in the group needs to pursue to renew your mind. What resources does the group have for finding these various programs?

2. Pair off and promise to check each week with your partner about his reading and/or memory program throughout the balance of this study about Paul.

3. Close by singing together a song such as *Open the Eyes of My Heart, Lord,* or by reading together Psalm 119:33-37:

Teach me, LORD, the meaning of Your statutes, and I will always keep them. Help me understand Your instruction, and I will obey it and follow it with all my heart. Help me to stay on the path of your commands, for I take pleasure in it. Turn my heart to Your decrees and not to material gain. Turn my eyes from looking at what is worthless; give me life in Your ways.

Next Week

Next week we will consider how Paul gained acceptance into an understandably skeptical Christian community back in Jerusalem. We will see the courageous role played by Barnabas when he promoted Paul's acceptance by the church. We will also discuss our own need to have supporters like Barnabas and, in turn, to be supporters of others who need a true friend.

Scripture Notes

Acts 9:19-22

9:20 That Saul, as a representative from the Jewish opposition, would be invited to speak in the synagogues is not unusual. What was unexpected was his message! ***began proclaiming Jesus ... is the Son of God.*** While this title is alluded to in only one other place in the Book of Acts (13:33), it is one of Paul's favorite ways of describing Jesus in the epistles.

9:21-22 The shocked reaction of the Jews in Damascus is understandable given their previous understanding of why Saul came to the city.

9:22 ***proving that this One is the Messiah.*** This was undoubtedly done by pointing out Old Testament passages about the Messiah that were fulfilled in the life and ministry of Jesus (Acts 8:34-35).

1:12 revelation. It was only after Jesus Christ revealed the truth and meaning of these facts to Paul following the Damascus Road experience that he accepted the gospel.

1:15 from my mother's womb set me apart. Paul's experience was similar to that of Old Testament prophets (Isa. 49:1-6; Jer. 1:5). He could see the hand of God throughout his life.

1:16 among the Gentiles. With Paul's conversion came his commission to preach to the Gentiles (Acts 9:15). In encountering Christ, he came to the realization that the Law was bankrupt (insofar as its ability to save anyone). There was no barrier preventing Gentiles from coming to the all-sufficient Christ.

FINDING A BRIDGE

LAST WEEK

Last week we examined the radical transformation that occurred in Paul's life immediately following his conversion to Christianity. We noted that, like Paul, we all undergo a significant spiritual transformation as the Holy Spirit conforms us to the image of Christ. We also noted that, unlike Paul, our transformation usually occurs in stages over a long period of time.

ICEBREAKER

Friendships enrich us. Many of our friendships grow out of common interests and shared perspectives on life. A few friendships grow out of a need for assistance. In some cases, we befriend someone who needs our help. In others, someone befriends us because we need his help. God values those kinds of relationships.

1. Who has made the biggest impact on you as a mentor and friend?
   a. A teacher or trainer
   b. An employer
   c. A counselor or accountability partner
   d. A military officer
   e. Other _____

2. In which of these capacities have you helped someone as a mentor and friend? How did you help?
   a. A coach
   b. A teacher or trainer
   c. An employer
   d. A counselor or accountability partner
   e. A military officer
   f. Other _____

3. Which of these statements best expresses your feelings about giving and receiving help? Why?
   a. I like to give help, but I'm uncomfortable receiving it.
   b. I'm comfortable giving and receiving help as an expression of love.
   c. I'm not very good at either one.

Paul experienced a lot of rejection once he became a follower of Christ. His former friends who remained committed to Pharisaic Judaism became his bitter enemies. Unfortunately, the Christians in Jerusalem and other cities of Judea did not believe he was truly one of them. Paul's behavior had been so malicious toward believers that they would not risk any kind of association with him.

However, God had a plan to help the Christian community accept Paul, particularly when he returned to Jerusalem after his three-year stay in Arabia. It all began with one man who took time to get to know Paul, befriend him, and then build a bridge to the apostles.

Needing a Friend

22 But Saul grew more capable, and kept confounding the Jews who lived in Damascus by proving that this One is the Messiah. 23 After many days had passed, the Jews conspired to kill him, 24 but their plot became known to Saul. So they were watching the gates day and night intending to kill him, 25 but his disciples took him by night and lowered him in a large basket through [an opening in] the wall.

Acts 9:22-25

32 In Damascus, the governor under King Aretas guarded the city of the Damascenes in order to arrest me, 33 so I was let down in a basket through a window in the wall and escaped his hands.

2 Corinthians 11:32-33

26 When he arrived in Jerusalem, he tried to associate with the disciples, but they were all afraid of him, since they did not believe he was a disciple. 27 Barnabas, however, took him and brought him to the apostles and explained to them how, on the road, Saul had seen the Lord, and that He had talked to him, and how in Damascus he had spoken boldly in the name of Jesus. 28 Saul was coming and going with them in Jerusalem, speaking boldly in the name of the Lord. 29 He conversed and debated with the Hellenistic Jews, but they attempted to kill him. 30 When the brothers found out, they took him down to Caesarea and sent him off to Tarsus. 31 So the church throughout all Judea, Galilee, and Samaria had peace, being built up and walking in the fear of the Lord and in the encouragement of the Holy Spirit, and it increased in numbers.

Acts 9:26-31

18 Then after three years I did go up to Jerusalem to get to know Cephas, and I stayed with him 15 days. 19 But I didn't see any of the other apostles except James, the Lord's brother. ...

²¹ Afterwards, I went to the regions of Syria and Cilicia. ²² I remained personally unknown to the Judean churches in Christ; ²³ they simply kept hearing: "He who formerly persecuted us now preaches the faith he once tried to destroy." ²⁴ And they glorified God because of me.

Galatians 1:18-19,21-24

PRINCIPLES TO LIVE BY

The following principles focus on Barnabas and his relationship with Paul. Humanly speaking, without Barnabas, Paul would never have received a hearing in Jerusalem.

PRINCIPLE 1

EVERYONE NEEDS TO FIND THEIR "BARNABAS." THIS IS A PERSON WHO BELIEVES IN US EVEN WHEN OTHERS DON'T. OUR "BARN-ABAS" IS ALSO THERE FOR US DURING THOSE TIMES WHEN WE DOUBT OUR OWN ABILITIES.

Paul returned to Damascus after spending nearly three years in Arabia discovering the messianic nature of the Old Testament and receiving revelation about justification by faith and the inclusion of Gentiles in the church of Jesus Christ. He once again used the Jewish synagogues as a platform for preaching the gospel.

However, Paul's message had deepened. He had definitely become more theologically astute. He was now able to prove from Scripture "that this One is the Messiah" (Acts 9:22). Paul preached with such deep passion, intense conviction, and depth of insight that he was "confounding the Jews who lived in Damascus." Nevertheless, they refused to repent. Paul should not have been surprised at the reaction of the Jews. His own pre-conversion behavior should have prepared him for rejection. He may even have anticipated that anger and frustration would soon lead the Jewish leaders to plot his death (v. 23).

When Paul learned of the assassination plot, he went into hiding while the other believers hatched their own scheme to spirit him safely, if not ignominiously, out of Damascus. They stuffed Paul into a large basket and lowered him with ropes from a window in the city wall.

Paul left Damascus knowing that the Jews and the governing authorities of the city wanted him dead (Acts 9:23; 2 Cor. 11:32). Then, when he arrived in Jerusalem, the Christians would have nothing to do with him because they doubted the reports of his conversion (Acts 9:26). Paul was a man in desperate need of a friend.

That friend appeared in the person of Barnabas. Barnabas found out quickly about Paul's sudden return to Jerusalem and made time to meet with him face-to-face. Though we don't know what transpired at this meeting, we can say with certainty that Barnabas believed Paul was for real. More importantly, Barnabas risked his reputation and championed Paul to the apostles and the rest of the church. He paved the way for Paul to enter the Christian community in Jerusalem.

We all face times when we need help, especially with things we can't do for ourselves. Sometimes we need others to open doors of access into groups we can't enter by ourselves and to vouch for our character and faith. God expects His people to follow the example of Barnabas: giving each other special support and encouragement.

PRINCIPLE 2

GOD WANTS US TO BE "ENCOURAGERS," PEOPLE WILLING TO TAKE RISKS AND INVEST TIME, TALENTS, AND TREASURES IN THE LIVES OF OTHERS.

Barnabas willingly risked his standing in the Jerusalem church to bring Paul into fellowship with the other believers. He firmly believed Paul's testimony. Barnabas walked so closely with God that the Holy Spirit certainly bore witness to him testifying that Paul was indeed telling the truth.

Paul wrote twice to the Thessalonians that Christians are to encourage one another and build each other up (1 Thess. 4:18; 5:11). Barnabas illustrated several ways we can encourage others:
- By sharing our material possessions generously and unselfishly
- By using our talents and abilities to build up other members of the body of Jesus Christ
- By being available and giving our time to get to know others and the needs in their lives.

PRINCIPLE 3

GOD WANTS US TO EXPRESS APPRECIATION TO OUR ENCOURAGERS SO THAT THEY MAY BE ENCOURAGED THEMSELVES.

Most of us have had men serve in the Barnabas role in our lives. We don't want to be one of those who has been mentored and given a leg up by a Barnabas only to plow ahead as though he had done it all on his own. It's tragic when we leave behind a Barnabas without a word of recognition or gratitude. Never forget your Barnabas! A note, an e-mail, or a telephone call to let your mentor know you hold him in high esteem because he encouraged you will in turn encourage your encourager.

WE MUST UNDERSTAND OURSELVES SO THAT WE KNOW IN WHAT AREAS WE ARE STRONG AND WEAK IN OUR ABILITY TO MAINTAIN RELATIONSHIPS.

Some of us are highly relational and love to be with people. Encouraging others comes naturally. Barnabas was probably this sort of man. Others of us are more comfortable with projects rather than people. Reaching out and encouraging others takes conscious effort and great determination.

Whether you are a people person or a project person, you can love others in ways that go beyond your natural abilities when you walk in the Spirit and allow God to control your life. Paul seems to have been a tough-minded, task-oriented, vision-casting leader. However, when he ministered in a local church, he could—by God's grace—be a gentle encourager (1 Thess. 2:7-8,11-12).

QUESTIONS FOR INTERACTION

1. When you face persistent opposition, do you tend to get discouraged or do you draw energy from that opposition?

2. How many points of possible discouragement do you see Paul facing in the Scriptures from this lesson?

3. Who had joined forces to dispose of Paul in Damascus (Acts 9:23; 2 Cor. 11:32)?

4. How did Paul have to depend on others to escape the assassination plot in Damascus (Acts 9:25; 2 Cor. 11:33)?

5. What do you suppose the Jerusalem Christians feared from Paul (Acts 9:26)?

6. Why do you suppose Barnabas championed Paul to the church and the apostles (v. 27)?

7. What did Barnabas accomplish for Paul by speaking up for him?

8. How did Paul's experience in Jerusalem parallel his experience in Damascus (vv. 29-30)?

9. What was the result of Paul's ministry in Jerusalem and departure to Tarsus (Acts 9:31; Gal. 1:22-24)?

10. How can the encouragement you give to others bring glory to God?

GOING DEEPER

11. Are you more of a people person or a project person? How does this affect your tendency to be an encourager?

12. Which of these best expresses how you encourage others? (You may choose more than one, as long as you identify which is your dominant form of helping.)
    a. Time—I listen well and encourage others with attention and advice.
    b. Talent—I have skills I can use to do helpful projects for others.
    c. Treasure—I have resources I like to give to assist others.

13. Did you ever express appreciation to the mentor/friend you identified in the Icebreaker? How could you thank that person or honor his or her memory now?

CARING TIME

This lesson challenges us to encourage others and to honor those who encourage us. Paul wrote to the Thessalonians, "Therefore encourage one another and build each other up as you are already doing" (1 Thess. 5:11). Take some time now to encourage one another through sharing and prayer.

1. Who in this group has encouraged you in the past? How did he do it?

2. How could we become more intentional about giving encouragement to one another in our group?

3. What discouraging situations are you facing that we can remember in our prayer time?

Next Week

Next week we will undertake some difficult "detective work" as we piece together from bits of the New Testament (and at times from between its lines) what Paul was up to during the half dozen years he spent in Tarsus before his public ministry began. By the time Paul joined Barnabas at Antioch (Acts 11:25-26), he had been a Christian nine years. While in Tarsus, he endured the disapproval of his family and neighbors who had expected him to take a different path in life. Family expectations can be hard to live with.

Scripture Notes

Acts 9:22-31

9:22 The shocked reaction of the Jews in Damascus is understandable given their previous understanding of why Saul had come to the city.

9:22 proving that this One is the Messiah. This was undoubtedly done by pointing out Old Testament passages about the Messiah that were fulfilled in the life and ministry of Jesus (Acts 8:34-35).

9:23 After many days had passed. When Saul next returned to Damascus, the leaders of the synagogues were prepared for him. Perhaps under accusations that his teaching was causing an uproar in the Jewish community, the leaders were able to draw upon the help of the governor of the city in a plot to capture Saul so that they might kill him (2 Cor. 11:32-33).

9:25 [an opening in] the wall. Ancient cities were surrounded by walls as a defense against enemies. Although the city gates were being closely observed, Saul escaped from the city by being lowered over the wall in a large basket. When Saul told of this incident in 2 Corinthians 11:32-33, it is in the context of describing the weakness and humiliation he had experienced as an apostle.

9:27 Barnabas. Barnabas took on an important role later as Paul's companion on his missionary trips. How Barnabas knew the reality of Paul's story is not explained, but it is clear he risked alienating himself from the church by siding with this former persecutor (Acts 4:36).

2 Corinthians 11:32-33

11:32 King Aretas. Aretas IV was a Nabataean Arab king who ruled from 9 B.C. to A.D. 40. In the first century, Nabataeans had extended their political power from the south (where Petra was their capital) all the way to Damascus.

GALATIANS 1:18-19,21-24

1:18 after three years. A significant interval of time elapsed between Paul's conversion and his first visit to Jerusalem. **Jerusalem**. It was a courageous act by Paul to return here—to his former friends who might well try to harm him (because of his conversion to Christianity), and to new friends who might not even receive him (because of their suspicions about him). **15 days**. This was a short visit, and Paul spent much of his time preaching (Acts 9:28-29).

1:19 James. James, the half brother of Jesus, eventually became the leader of the Jerusalem church (Mark 6:3; Acts 1:14).

1:21 Syria and Cilicia. After leaving Jerusalem, Paul went north into Syria and then into the adjacent area of Cilicia to the city of Tarsus, his birthplace.

Strange Homecoming

Last Week

Last week we noted that Paul needed certain friends in order to succeed in the ministry to which God called him. Ananias served as God's channel to restore Paul's sight and relay God's predictions about his future. Certain disciples in Damascus saved Paul's life by lowering him through the city wall to safety. In Jerusalem, Barnabas championed Paul to the skeptical apostles and church. Without friends from God, Paul's lifework could not have gotten off the ground.

Icebreaker

We live in a culture that grows increasingly diverse in its religious attitudes and beliefs. Fifty to a hundred years ago, most western nations reflected Christian cultural values and traditions. Now we see secular forces pressuring public and private institutions to remove every vestige of cultural Christianity and trying to restrict the rights of devout individuals to express their religious views. Under the banner of "tolerance," the world is becoming increasingly hostile to people who share their faith with others.

1. What was the spiritual climate of the family in which you grew up?
   a. Dedicated believers in Christ
   b. Nominally Christian
   c. Observed a non-Christian religion
   d. Indifferent to spiritual values
   e. Hostile to Christianity or any religion

2. How are your Christian values regarded by your extended family?
   a. Shared
   b. Respected
   c. Tolerated
   d. Resisted
   e. Belittled
   f. Attacked

3. Share something about what you've seen of religions in other parts of the world.

One of the most difficult places to share the message of salvation is among those who know us best. When Jesus returned to Nazareth early in His ministry, local residents scoffed at Him because they had known Him from boyhood. Jesus observed, "I assure you: No prophet is accepted in his hometown" (Luke 4:24). When Paul returned to the familiar and beloved environs of Tarsus, fresh from ego-bruising rejection in Damascus and Jerusalem, he discovered the special kind of persecution "prophets" face in their hometowns.

Strong Jewish Roots

3 He continued, "I am a Jewish man, born in Tarsus of Cilicia, but brought up in this city at the feet of Gamaliel, and educated according to the strict view of our patriarchal law. Being zealous for God, just as all of you are today."

Acts 22:3

5 Circumcised the eighth day; of the nation of Israel, of the tribe of Benjamin, a Hebrew born of Hebrews; as to the law, a Pharisee; 6 as to zeal, persecuting the church; as to the righteousness that is in the law, blameless.

Philippians 3:5-6

Sent Home Changed

17 "After I came back to Jerusalem and was praying in the temple complex, I went into a visionary state 18 and saw Him telling me, 'Hurry and get out of Jerusalem quickly, because they will not accept your testimony about Me!'
19 "But I said, 'Lord, they know that in synagogue after synagogue I had those who believed in You imprisoned and beaten. 20 And when the blood of Your witness Stephen was being shed, I myself was standing by and approving, and I guarded the clothes of those who killed him.'
21 "Then He said to me, 'Go, because I will send you far away to the Gentiles.' "

Acts 22:17-21

28 Saul was coming and going with them in Jerusalem, speaking boldly in the name of the Lord. 29 He conversed and debated with the Hellenistic Jews, but they attempted to kill him. 30 When the brothers found out, they took him down to Caesarea and sent him off to Tarsus.

Acts 9:28-30

Abandoned?

¹² But to the rest I, not the Lord, say: If any brother has an unbelieving wife, and she is willing to live with him, he must not leave her. ¹³ Also, if any woman has an unbelieving husband, and he is willing to live with her, she must not leave her husband. ... ¹⁵ But if the unbeliever leaves, let him leave. A brother or a sister is not bound in such cases. God has called you to peace.

1 Corinthians 7:12-13,15

Hardships

²⁴ Five times I received from the Jews 40 lashes minus one. ...
²⁵ Three times I was shipwrecked.
I have spent a night and a day in the depths of the sea.

2 Corinthians 11:24,25b

Exalted and Abased

² I know a man in Christ who was caught up into the third heaven 14 years ago. Whether he was in the body or out of the body, I don't know; God knows. ³ I know that this man—whether in the body or out of the body I do not know, God knows— ⁴ was caught up into paradise. He heard inexpressible words, which a man is not allowed to speak. ... ⁷ Therefore, so that I would not exalt myself, a thorn in the flesh was given to me, a messenger of Satan to torment me so I would not exalt myself. ⁸ Concerning this, I pleaded with the Lord three times to take it away from me. ⁹ But He said to me, "My grace is sufficient for you, for power is perfected in weakness." Therefore, I will most gladly boast all the more about my weaknesses, so that Christ's power may reside in me. ¹⁰ So because of Christ, I am pleased in weaknesses, in insults, in catastrophes, in persecutions, and in pressures. For when I am weak, then I am strong.

2 Corinthians 12:2-4,7-10

²⁵ Then he [Barnabas] went to Tarsus to search for Saul, ²⁶ and when he found him he brought him to Antioch. For a whole year they met with the church and taught large numbers, and the disciples were first called Christians in Antioch.

Acts 11:25-26

PRINCIPLES TO LIVE BY

Paul spent a half dozen or so years in Tarsus (roughly A.D. 38-44). The suffering he undoubtedly underwent through those silent years of preparation and ministry should cause us to reflect soberly on our own witness to family and friends whom we love. It should also challenge us to remember and pray for the millions of believers around the world who live and serve in hostile settings.

At the time of Paul's conversion, the Lord had revealed to him through Ananias that he would suffer much for the name of Jesus (Acts 9:16). That prophecy started coming true right away. After Paul's time of seclusion in Arabia, the Jews of Damascus tried to kill him (v. 23). When he escaped to Jerusalem, the Jews plotted to kill him there, too (v. 29).

The believers in Jerusalem sent Paul to his home city, Tarsus, so that he could avoid further persecution (v. 30). This led to peace for the Jerusalem church (v. 31), but not for Paul. The Damascus and Jerusalem experiences were very, very difficult; however, both would pale in his memory compared with the intense, persistent persecution he would receive in Tarsus.

Paul's family, fellow rabbis, and the whole Jewish community received the shock of their lives when he returned. No doubt they had heard about his conversion to Christianity, but they were not prepared for the radical change in his life and the extent of his redirected zeal.

It had cost Paul's father dearly to send his son to study under Gamaliel. He had a lot invested in Paul's climb up the ladder of leadership in Judaism. When he discovered that Paul had renounced Judaism, he was shamed. He had two choices—either he could follow Paul in accepting Jesus as the Messiah or he could disown and disinherit Paul as his son. The latter option is probably what occurred. Paul found himself cut off from his family and from any prospect he had of inheriting the family fortune.

According to the rabbis, every dedicated Jewish father wanted three things for his son: knowledge of the Law, a good trade, and a virtuous wife. Paul had achieved the first two. Did he have a wife? Some Bible scholars speculate Paul was alluding to his own experience when he wrote, "If any brother has an unbelieving wife, and she is willing to live with him, he must not leave her. ... But if the unbeliever leaves, let him leave. A brother or a sister is not bound in such cases" (1 Cor. 7:12,15a).

We should not be surprised when non-Christian parents or siblings don't want to hear the gospel from us. Sometimes the very intensity of our longing to see them come to faith annoys and alienates family members. They often resent hearing their son or brother saying they are sinners needing a Savior.

That doesn't relieve us of the obligation to share the gospel sensitively and lovingly. Sometimes we have to shift to a nonverbal pattern of reflecting the fruit of the Holy Spirit and waiting and praying for a time when they will ask us why we have the hope in Christ that we do (1 Pet. 3:15-16).

PRINCIPLE 2

WE WILL DO WELL TO REMEMBER PAST BELIEVERS WHO SUFFERED SO THAT WE MAY EXPERIENCE THE FREEDOM INHERENT IN JESUS CHRIST.

Paul's struggles are chronicled in the New Testament as a matter of record and as a part of the over-arching story of his ministry. But even more than that, his trials have been preserved so that we can have additional testimony to the cost of obedience. Paul and other Christians from the past have given much so that we may know and better understand the gospel of Jesus Christ.

Paul did not quit proclaiming Christ when his family rejected him and his childhood friends wanted nothing to do with him. He evidently engaged regularly in reading and expounding the Old Testament in the synagogues. We get hints about the reaction of the Jews of Tarsus from Paul's second letter to the Corinthians. In chapters 11 and 12, Paul tells of several hardships he had endured. Some refer to incidents contained in the Book of Acts. One occurred 14 years before Paul wrote to Corinth (2 Cor. 12:2). That would have been A.D. 42, right in the middle of Paul's stay in Tarsus. Others also probably occurred while Paul was at Tarsus.

Paul said he was beaten with 39 lashes on five occasions (11:24). Judaism had incorporated flogging into its methods of maintaining synagogue discipline. During the half dozen years Paul stayed at Tarsus he provoked the most extreme form of discipline various local assemblies could administer on several occasions.

During this time, Paul experienced shipwreck three times, once spending a night and a day at sea clinging to wreckage and awaiting rescue (11:25b). Perhaps after he had been excommunicated from the synagogues of Tarsus, Paul began cruising the coastline of Cilicia in small ships in order to preach to Gentiles. At any rate, Paul endured the harrowing hazards of first-century sea travel.

It is hard for most of us to imagine being persecuted or suffering hardships for proclaiming Christ, but Paul suffered terribly to bring the gospel to his fellow Jews and the Gentiles. We only enjoy the freedoms we do today because courageous Christians endured opposition and hardship for centuries until western civilization became Christianized. We should desire to display the same courage in a post-Christian culture that is once again displaying hostility to faith in Jesus Christ.

WE SHOULD PRAY CONTINUALLY FOR BELIEVERS WHO SUFFER AS A RESULT OF THEIR BELIEF IN AND WITNESS FOR JESUS CHRIST.

During the years he spent at Tarsus, Paul learned to suffer patiently for the gospel of Jesus Christ. He never became a fatalist. In later years, he called on the Corinthians to pray for him and his fellow missionaries as they faced frightening "affliction ... in the province of Asia" (2 Cor. 1:8). When Paul and his companions faced this kind of persecution, he admitted that he wasn't sure of its outcome. He knew that they might lose their lives, but even if they did he knew they would be delivered, "whether by life or by death" (Phil. 1:20).

Do we have a responsibility to pray for persecuted believers around the world, even though we don't know who they are? Definitely! And prayer does change things. Though they may not be delivered from persecution, they will find strength to face even death victoriously and experience ultimate deliverance into the very presence of the God they love and serve.

PRINCIPLE 4

WE SHOULD PRAY CONTINUALLY FOR OUR LEADERSHIP—GOVERNMENT, CIVIC, PROFESSIONAL—SO THAT WE MIGHT LIVE IN PEACE AND SHARE THE GOSPEL OF JESUS CHRIST.

Paul wrote Timothy urging that prayers be offered "for kings and all those who are in authority, so that we may lead a tranquil and quiet life" (1 Tim. 2:2). Paul recognized that his life of persecution and hardship is not necessarily what God wants for His people. God's will is that we live in an environment of freedom from persecution so we will have opportunity to present the gospel to many people (vv. 3-4). We should pray for those with leadership responsibilities in every culture so they will lead their nations in a way that will give all people this kind of freedom.

QUESTIONS FOR INTERACTION

1. Which member of your family would you most like to see come to faith in Christ or renew his or her relationship with Him?

2. How do you think Paul felt about the salvation of his fellow Jews?

3. From what Paul said of his Jewish roots (Acts 22:3; Phil. 3:5-6), who would his friends have been and where would they have lived?

4. Why would those friends have had a hard time accepting Paul's conversion to faith in Christ?

5. What were the human and the divine explanations for Paul's departure from Jerusalem for Tarsus (Acts 9:28-30; 22:17-21)?

6. What hardships did Paul likely experience within his immediate family during the years he was in Tarsus?

7. What ministry-related persecutions did Paul probably experience during the years he was in Tarsus (2 Cor. 11:24,25b)?

8. How do you suppose Paul's revelation and attendant "thorn in the flesh" helped him keep the right perspective through all the difficulties of his years in Tarsus (2 Cor. 12:2-4,7-10)?

9. By A.D. 44, roughly 10 years had passed since Paul met the Lord on the Damascus Road. What do you suppose Paul thought about the prophecy that he himself would "carry [Christ's] name before Gentiles, kings, and the sons of Israel?" What about the assurance to Paul from Jesus, " I will certainly show him how much he must suffer for My name" (Acts 9:15-16)?

10. What is God teaching you about His ways through the positive or negative spiritual climate of your family?

GOING DEEPER

11. Whom do you look to as historical or contemporary heroes because of how they withstood persecution in order to express their belief in Christ?

12. Which missionaries do you most admire for his or her courage and grace under pressure? Why?

13. In your opinion, what part of the world most needs to have the gospel of Christ proclaimed and accepted? Why?

Caring Time

This lesson gives us the opportunity to pray for one another's families and for parts of the world where the gospel is opposed and Christians are persecuted. It is a good thing to do this in the group setting. It is a better thing to remember these concerns and pray regularly for them through the days and weeks ahead.

1. Which of your family members, in addition to the one you mentioned during "Questions for Interaction," need to trust Jesus as Savior?

2. What barriers do you face in trying to share Christ within your extended family?

3. Pray for the man to your left concerning his unbelieving family members and any region of the world for which he expressed concern.

Next Week

Next week we will see how the Lord launched the gospel of Christ from its Jewish roots out into the larger Gentile world. He intentionally used Peter, the apostle to the Jews, to lead the first group of Gentiles into a saving relationship with Jesus. Once the Jewish church overcame its prejudice against the Gentiles and admitted that God had responded to their faith, God put Barnabas and Paul together and started training them to be His first official emissaries to the Gentiles.

Scripture Notes

Acts 9:28-30; 11:25-26; 22:3,17-21

11:26 the disciples were first called Christians. By the time of Luke's writing, this Latin term was a widespread name for the believers. Since the only other places in the New Testament where this term is used were situations of ridicule and persecution (Acts 26:28; 1 Pet. 4:16), it may have been originally a name used to mock the believers.

22:3 a Jewish man ... brought up in this city. Although a citizen of Tarsus by virtue of his birth, Paul had spent most of his early life in Jerusalem. Chapter 23:16 implies that Paul's sister and her family lived in the city. *Gamaliel*. Gamaliel was a highly respected Pharisee, head of the Hillel wing of this sect. To have received an education from this man was to have had access to the best possible Jewish education (Acts 5:34). *our patriarchal law*. Paul emphasized that he too had a lifelong knowledge of and respect for the Law.

1 CORINTHIANS 7:12-13,15

7:12-13 Paul examined the issue of marriage to a non-Christian spouse. A Christian is not to take the initiative to divorce his or her non-believing spouse.

7:15 But should the non-Christian partner leave, the prohibition against divorce does not apply.

2 CORINTHIANS 11:24,25B; 12:2-4,7-10

11:25b shipwrecked. One shipwreck is described in Acts 27:14-44, but that had not yet occurred when Paul wrote 2 Corinthians. Since Paul traveled frequently by ship and since shipwrecks were by no means uncommon in those days, it seems that Paul endured several shipwrecks, some of them during his years of ministry around Tarsus.

12:2 caught up. Visions were often spoken of in terms of a journey to another place. Whether Paul was literally transported to a new place or simply found himself in a new reality is impossible to know. **third heaven.** Jewish literature spoke of heaven having various levels, although the number of levels differs. **14 years ago.** This was probably around A.D. 42, well before Paul planted the Corinthian church. This is the only time in any letter that Paul mentioned such an experience. **in the body or out of the body.** Paul refused to speculate on how this experience occurred.

12:7 a thorn in the flesh. It is unknown what Paul meant here. **messenger of Satan.** Sickness was thought to be caused by Satan, but the false apostles in Corinth were also referred to as servants of Satan (2 Cor. 11:13-15). **torment me.** Literally, "to continually torment me." Whatever the problem was, it was chronic, though not debilitating.

12:8 three times. There are parallels between Paul's experience and that of Jesus in the Garden of Gethsemane. Like Jesus, Paul was not delivered of the hardship that faced him but received strength to remain faithful in the midst of suffering.

12:9 The false teachers and the Corinthians thought that the power of God caused Christians to escape or avoid all encounters with weakness, vulnerability, suffering, and hardship that are common to life. Paul emphasized that the power of God does not keep believers from trials but empowers them to love, bring healing, serve, and be faithful in the midst of such times (2 Cor. 1:3-11).

3:5 eighth day. It was on the eighth day after birth that a Jewish baby boy (as opposed to an adult proselyte) was circumcised. Paul was a true Jew right from the time of his birth. *the tribe of Benjamin*. The members of the tribe of Benjamin constituted an elite group within Israel. *a Pharisee*. He was one of the spiritual elite in Israel.

3:6 as to zeal, persecuting the church. Zeal was a highly prized virtue among the Jews. Paul had demonstrated his zeal for the law by ferreting out Christians and bringing them to trial (Acts 22:4-5; 26:9-11). *blameless*. To the best of his ability, Paul tried to observe the whole Law. Taken together, all these attributes mean that Paul was in every way the match of his Jewish opponents in Philippi who belittled his qualifications to speak authoritatively about spiritual issues. He had lived at the very pinnacle of Judaism.

SEEING BEYOND THE FAMILIAR

LAST WEEK

Last week we considered the hardships Paul must have experienced during the six years he spent at Tarsus between the time he left Jerusalem and emerged as a missionary to the Gentiles. His family and friends probably rejected him. The Jewish community persecuted him for his faith in Christ. He suffered physical hardships as he began to travel and evangelize the Gentiles. Paul's experiences should remind us to pray for Christians today who live in hostile settings and suffer for their faith.

ICEBREAKER

Prejudice is one of the unfortunate results of living in a sinful world. Too often we deal with our insecurities and fears by belittling groups around us by whom we feel threatened or that we just don't understand. For instance, in school the "jocks" hate the "geeks" (after all, they're going to work for them all their adult lives), and there are plenty that can't stand cheerleaders or those that may belong to certain clubs.

Big-city dwellers who use public transportation distrust suburbanites who drive SUVs. Nobody likes New York Yankee fans, except other Yankee fans (just kidding, sort of). And that's all on top of the biggies—racial, sexual, social, economic, and age prejudices!

1. When you were growing up, what individuals or groups did people look down upon in your neighborhood ?

2. What groups were you a part of when you were in high school? Whom did your groups look down upon? Who looked down on you?

3. Which of these experiences had the greatest effect on helping you appreciate the differences among people? How?
   a. College
   b. Military service
   c. Athletics
   d. Travel
   e. Church life
   f. Other _____

About five years had passed since the Day of Pentecost. The church was growing rapidly throughout this period, but it was a uniquely Jewish church. In spite of Jesus' Great Commission to take the gospel to all the nations, the apostles and the church had not considered that Gentiles could be saved without first converting to Judaism.

To change that perception, the Holy Spirit zeroed in on Peter, the primary leader of the apostles. The Spirit used extraordinary means to convince Peter that God accepted Gentiles based on their faith alone. Peter, in turn, didn't hesitate to defend his "startling" discovery to the church at Jerusalem.

Coming Clean

[9] Peter went up to pray on the housetop at about noon. [10] Then he became hungry and wanted to eat, but while they were preparing something he went into a visionary state. [11] He saw heaven opened and an object coming down that resembled a large sheet being lowered to the earth by its four corners. [12] In it were all the four-footed animals and reptiles of the earth, and the birds of the sky. [13] Then a voice said to him, "Get up, Peter; kill and eat!"

[14] "No, Lord!" Peter said. "For I have never eaten anything common and unclean!"

[15] Again, a second time, a voice said to him, "What God has made clean, you must not call common." [16] This happened three times, and then the object was taken up into heaven.

[17] While Peter was deeply perplexed about what the vision he had seen might mean, the men who had been sent by Cornelius, having asked directions to Simon's house, stood at the gate. [18] They called out, asking if Simon, who was also named Peter, was lodging there. ...

[23] The next day he got up and set out with them, and some of the brothers from Joppa went with him. [24] The following day he entered Caesarea. Now Cornelius was expecting them and had called together his relatives and close friends. ... [28] Peter said to them, "You know it's forbidden for a Jewish man to associate with or visit a foreigner. But God has shown me that I must not call any person common or unclean." ...

[34] Then Peter began to speak: "In truth, I understand that God doesn't show favoritism, [35] but in every nation the person who fears Him and does righteousness is acceptable to Him." ...

[44] While Peter was still speaking these words, the Holy Spirit came down on all those who heard the message. [45] The circumcised believers who had come with Peter were astounded, because the gift of the Holy Spirit had been poured out on the Gentiles also. [46] For they heard them speak-

ing in [other] languages and declaring the greatness of God.
Then Peter responded, [47] "Can anyone withhold water and prevent these from being baptized, who have received the Holy Spirit just as we have?" [48] And he commanded them to be baptized in the name of Jesus Christ. Then they asked him to stay for a few days.
[1] The apostles and the brothers who were throughout Judea heard that the Gentiles had welcomed God's message also. [2] When Peter went up to Jerusalem, those who stressed circumcision argued with him, [3] saying, "You visited uncircumcised men and ate with them!"
[4] Peter began to explain to them in an orderly sequence. ... [18] When they heard this they became silent. Then they glorified God, saying, "So God has granted repentance resulting in life to even the Gentiles!"
[19] Those who had been scattered as a result of the persecution that started because of Stephen made their way as far as Phoenicia, Cyprus, and Antioch, speaking the message to no one except Jews. [20] But there were some of them, Cypriot and Cyrenian men, who came to Antioch and began speaking to the Hellenists, proclaiming the good news about the Lord Jesus. [21] The Lord's hand was with them, and a large number who believed turned to the Lord. [22] Then the report about them reached the ears of the church in Jerusalem, and they sent out Barnabas to travel as far as Antioch. [23] When he arrived and saw the grace of God, he was glad, and he encouraged all of them to remain true to the Lord with a firm resolve of the heart— [24] for he was a good man, full of the Holy Spirit and of faith—and large numbers of people were added to the Lord. [25] Then he went to Tarsus to search for Saul, [26] and when he found him he brought him to Antioch. For a whole year they met with the church and taught large numbers, and the disciples were first called Christians in Antioch. ...
[28] A severe famine throughout the Roman world ... took place during the time of Claudius. [29] So each of the disciples, according to his ability, determined to send relief to the brothers who lived in Judea. [30] This they did, sending it to the elders by means of Barnabas and Saul.

Acts 10:9b-18,23b-24,28,34-35,44-48; 11:1-4,18-26,28b-30

PRINCIPLES TO LIVE BY

Pride and Prejudice is more than the title of a Jane Austin novel. "Pride" and "prejudice" are twin sins that lurk in every soul. To some extent, all of us have prejudices woven into the fabric of our personalities. We don't think about them; we think with them. We have trouble looking at them, because they are lenses through which we look at all of life.

Our prejudices—our petty feelings of superiority to certain kinds of people—die hard. We can think prejudice is gone, only to find ourselves patronizing "those poor people" whom we fear will never make it on their own. It seems the need for the renewing of our minds will go on as long as we live in the flesh.

PRINCIPLE 1

MOST PEOPLE IN THE WORLD, INCLUDING CHRISTIANS, ARE INFECTED WITH THE SUBTLE, SOCIAL DISEASE CALLED PREJUDICE.

The only thing more unsettling to Peter than associating with Gentiles was eating food declared unclean by the Law. The Jews looked at the Gentiles with an outright disdain. Although Peter argued with God when he was told to eat unclean food (Acts 10:14), once he got the idea that God could change his stance about unclean food, Peter found it possible to imagine God accepting "unclean" people (v. 28). This event destroyed Peter's perspective on these issues and moved him a long way down the road toward abandoned prejudice.

The Jerusalem church reluctantly accepted Peter's report of Gentile conversions because of the vision Peter had seen and because the Holy Spirit clearly validated those conversions (11:4-10,15-17). However, it would take years for church policy to embrace Gentile converts enthusiastically. The New Testament occasionally alludes to persistent pockets of Jewish believers who taught that observance of the Law of Moses was necessary for the Christian life.

Paul wrote the Galatians, "There is no Jew or Greek, slave or free, male or female; for you are all one in Christ Jesus" (3:28). We could expand his words to include people from all cultures of the world. When we are in Christ, there is no black or white, rich or poor, Swede or Norwegian, German or Jew, CEO or clerk, or husband or wife. We are Christians, which means we are one body in Jesus Christ and members of one another (Rom. 12:4-5).

PRINCIPLE 2

OUR PREJUDICE IS SIN. WE MUST REPENT OF IT AND CONFESS IT TO GOD IN ORDER TO RECEIVE FORGIVENESS.

Even though Peter went out of his way to state that God had shown him he had been wrong to think of Gentiles as unclean (Acts 10:28,34-35; 11:17-18), early admissions of prejudice were tortured and reluctant (11:18). Prejudice is a difficult sin to face, but we must call it what it is. It is falling short of God's perfect standard and that is sin.

James, the half-brother of Jesus and the acknowledged leader of the Jerusalem church, confronted prejudice head on. No doubt he had a lot of experience with it in his own life and in the church he oversaw. James wrote, "If you really carry out the royal law prescribed in Scripture, 'Love your neighbor as yourself,' you are doing well. But if you show favoritism, you commit sin and are convicted by the law as transgressors" (James 2:8-9).

PRINCIPLE 3

WE MUST ALLOW THE HOLY SPIRIT TO WORK IN REMOVING OUR PREJUDICES THROUGH THE RENEWING OUR MINDS.

Like most sins, prejudice is rooted in our minds and expresses itself in how we think and feel about life. When we are prejudiced, we are "conformed to this age" (Rom. 12:2). Prejudicial thinking and behavior, therefore, is worldly and ingrained in us. However, when we capture our thoughts and direct them to what is true, honorable, just, pure, lovely, and commendable, we will find the Holy Spirit renewing our minds (Phil. 4:8). We will be able to walk in "the good, pleasing, and perfect will of God" (Rom. 12:2).

We are to "accept one another, just as the Messiah also accepted" us (15:7). How did Christ accept us? Without conditions. All people, regardless of their race, creed, ethnic background, economic status, and educational opportunities are welcome in the family of God.

We see the Holy Spirit renewing the minds of the Jewish church by sending visions, by validating the conversion of Cornelius' family, by blessing the church at Antioch, and by ministering through the church at Antioch to the Judean church. It had to be humbling and thought provoking for the Jewish Christians to accept aid in an hour of crisis from a largely Gentile church (Acts 11:29-30).

QUESTIONS FOR INTERACTION

1. What social, economic, political, or racial biases do you think may restrict the outreach of your church into your community?

2. What social, economic, political, or racial biases do you need to conquer within your own heart?

3. How had Peter's obsession for the Law turned to pride and prejudice?

4. How can our concern for holiness and separation from the world lead to pride and prejudice?

5. What did God do to break down Peter's prejudices against Gentiles (Acts 10:9-18; 11:44-48)?

6. How might God break down barriers of prejudice in your church?

7. Why were the Jewish believers from Cyprus and northern Africa more willing to reach out to Gentiles than the church in Jerusalem (Acts 11:19-21)?

8. Whom do you see setting the example for breaking down prejudices and reaching out to all sorts of people in your church?

9. How can you become more open to ministering to people you have tended to avoid?

Going Deeper

10. How can some Christians study the Bible and attend church for years but never deal with their personal prejudices?

11. What do you think ultimately happens to a church that is content to exclude certain people from its pews?

12. How do you think God "renews our minds" from prejudice? What are some of the processes involved?

Caring Time

This Caring Time provides an opportunity to share how our backgrounds affect our prejudices, how we have experienced prejudicial treatment, and how our faith affects our prejudices. This conversation may go in any number of directions. It could reveal deep wounds or conflicted emotions. It could reveal good progress toward renewed minds. Pray for one another that the Holy Spirit will continue the process of renewing your minds.

1. What biases have you experienced that were directed against you? How did that make you feel?
2. What prejudices did your family hold or teach (intentionally or unintentionally)? How have you tried to deal with these thoughts as you've grown older?

3. How has your faith in Christ changed your attitude toward those the world tends to reject and marginalize?

NEXT WEEK

Our focus next week will be on Paul's first missionary journey in the company of Barnabas and—for a while—John Mark, the writer of the Gospel of Mark. We will see Paul emerge from the shadow of Barnabas to become the natural leader of this outreach to Gentiles. God had called and gifted Paul for this kind of ministry, and we will observe how it quickly became apparent once the work began.

SCRIPTURE NOTES

ACTS 10:9B-28,34-35,44-48; 11:1-4,18-26-30

10:13 kill and eat. The voice invited Peter to partake of any of the animals in the sheet, but Peter protested that he had never violated the dietary laws of the Jews.

10:14 Lord! Typically in the Book of Acts, this word is used as a title for Jesus. Peter may have recognized his dream as coming from the Lord, but he was not willing simply to follow the Lord's invitation to eat of the food.

10:15 In Mark 7:19, Jesus laid the groundwork for the pronouncement that, despite the laws of Leviticus 11, food simply was not a spiritual issue. Such laws had their place earlier in Jewish history as a means of separating them from the pagans in neighboring areas. Peter soon came to see that if God could pronounce certain foods that were formerly unclean were now acceptable, He could do the same thing with people. If it was now acceptable for Jews to eat the food of Gentiles, then the Gentiles themselves would have to be considered as acceptable to God as well.

10:28 it's forbidden. Jews would not associate with Gentiles partly because of the problems associated with their dietary laws. To have such associations rendered the Jew ceremonially unclean and thus ineligible for worship at the temple until a length of time had passed and a prescribed ceremony of cleansing had been performed. Because Gentile food may have come from unclean animals or even from an animal that had been sacrificed as part of a pagan ritual, eating with them was especially taboo. ***foreigner.*** This Greek word, used only here in the New Testament, is the least offensive way possible for Jews to refer to Gentiles, as opposed to the derogatory term in 11:3 used by those upset with Peter. ***But God has shown me.*** Although the vision was about food, Peter caught on that its significance was about people. Culture, race, or physical condition does not make a person "unclean," but sinful behavior and unbelief does.

10:45 This phenomenon shocked Peter's companions as it violated all they had known about traditional divisions between Jews and Gentiles. It meant that the Gentiles were on equal terms with Jews before God.

10:46 Luke's mention of the fact that these Gentiles spoke in tongues was not meant to teach that this sign must always accompany the outpouring of the Sprit, but was needed to convince the Jewish believers that the Gentile's experience of the Spirit was no less real than that of the apostles.

10:47 Baptism with the Spirit usually accompanied (2:38,41) or followed (8:15-17) baptism with water. Had the Spirit not come at this point, the Jewish believers may have insisted that before Cornelius and his family and friends could be baptized as true followers of the Messiah, they must be circumcised and agree to observe Jewish traditions about food, the Sabbath, etc.

10:48 they asked him to stay for a few days. Violating custom once again, Peter, a Jew, accepted Gentile hospitality. This was another clear indication of his acceptance of them as full members of God's family.

11:2 those who stressed circumcision. At this point, all the believers (except Cornelius and his household) were circumcised. These would be Christians who were Jews.

11:18 While the Jerusalem church saw in principle that Gentiles were to be included in the church, tradition and prejudice kept Jewish believers from acting on that truth to any extent (chap. 15). Instead, it was the church at Antioch, to which Luke now turns his attention, that spearheaded the missionary movement.

11:19 Since there were Jewish communities throughout the Roman Empire, it is not unusual that the Jewish believers would have spread throughout such a large area. **Phoenicia.** Modern Lebanon. **Antioch.** Located about 300 miles north of Jerusalem, this was the capital of the Roman province of Syria. It was the third-largest city in the Roman Empire (after Rome and Alexandria), with a population estimated at 750,000, including a Jewish community of 25,000. A well-developed road system and access to a seaport made Antioch an important transportation and communication center. An early tradition teaches that Antioch was Luke's home.

11:20-21 These disciples from Cyprus and Cyrene were Jews who lived away from Judea and were used to interacting with Gentiles. Gentile God-fearers (like Cornelius) who were attracted to the ethics and values of Judaism while not accepting its customs regarding food, circumcision, and Sabbath regulations undoubtedly attended the synagogues in Antioch. It is probably with these Gentiles that the believers shared the gospel. From this sharing of the gospel, many believed.

11:23-24 Barnabas did not require the Gentile converts to submit to Jewish traditions, but only encouraged them to maintain a heartfelt loyalty to Jesus as Lord. This is the essence of Christian discipleship. His message, coupled with his character, drew many to faith.

11:26 the disciples were first called Christians. By the time of Luke's writing, this Latin term was a widespread name for the believers. Since the only other places in the New Testament where this term is used were situations of ridicule and persecution (Acts 26:28; 1 Pet. 4:16), it may have been originally a name used to mock the believers.

11:28 There was no single widespread famine during Claudius' reign (A.D. 41-54), but there were at least five localized famines during this period.

PREPARATION MEETS OPPORTUNITY

LAST WEEK

Last week we looked at the centuries-old prejudice of the Jews against the Gentiles. This prejudice was so strong that it prevented the early Jewish Christians from even thinking about preaching the gospel of Christ to non-Jews. We saw the great lengths God used to make it clear to Peter and the Jewish church that He intended to include Gentiles as equal partners with Jews in the body of Christ. That ancient prejudice is difficult for us to imagine, even as our own prejudices are difficult for us to admit and reject as sin. Nevertheless, we dishonor the Lord Jesus who loved and died for all people equally when we assume we are better than others.

ICEBREAKER

One of the ways children learn about life is by imitating adults. They imitate their parents. They imitate police officers, firefighters, soldiers, and cowboys. Most of us based our first idea about what we wanted to do when we grew up on what seemed exciting or daring.

1. When you were a small boy, what did you want to be when you grew up? Why?

2. By the time you were in high school, what did you want to be when you grew up? Why?

3. If expense, education, and experience weren't barriers, what career do you wish you could pursue? Why?

BIBLICAL FOUNDATION

Approximately 11 or 12 years after Paul's conversion, he was ready for his first missionary trip. God had been preparing him from birth. His family and synagogue education had grounded him in the Old Testament. His formal training under Gamaliel had taught him the rules of Pharisaic legalism. His exposure to Greek and Roman thought had familiarized him with secular philosophers and poets.

Paul's three-year stay in Arabia had deprogrammed him of the fanatical aspect of his zeal and integrated his Old Testament knowledge with both the teachings of Jesus and the revelations he had received about the gospel. In and around Tarsus, Paul had learned to persevere in the face of rejection, persecution, and hardship.

Finally, Barnabas had sought Paul out and taken him to Antioch in Syria where a church with a sizeable Gentile component was growing by leaps and bounds. For a year, Barnabas mentored Paul and taught him about building a church in an urban center.

Taking the Gospel on the Road

[1] In the local church at Antioch there were prophets and teachers ... . [2] As they were ministering to the Lord and fasting, the Holy Spirit said, "Set apart for Me Barnabas and Saul for the work that I have called them to."

[3] Then, after they had fasted, prayed, and laid hands on them, they sent them off.

[4] Being sent out by the Holy Spirit, they came down to Seleucia, and from there they sailed to Cyprus. [5] Arriving in Salamis, they proclaimed God's message in the Jewish synagogues. They also had John as their assistant. ...

[9] Then Saul—also called Paul—[was] filled with the Holy Spirit ... .

[13] Paul and his companions set sail from Paphos and came to Perga in Pamphylia. John, however, left them and went back to Jerusalem. [14] They continued their journey from Perga and reached Antioch in Pisidia. On the Sabbath day they went into the synagogue and sat down.

[15] After the reading of the Law and the Prophets, the leaders of the synagogue sent [word] to them, saying, "Brothers, if you have any message of encouragement for the people, you can speak."

[16] Then standing up, Paul motioned with his hand and spoke: ... [38] "Therefore, let it be known to you, brothers, that through this man forgiveness of sins is being proclaimed to you, [39] and everyone who believes in Him is justified from everything, which you could not be justified from through the law of Moses." ...

[42] As they were leaving, they begged that these matters be presented to them the following Sabbath. [43] After the synagogue had been dismissed, many of the Jews and devout proselytes followed Paul and Barnabas, who were speaking with them and persuading them to continue in the grace of God.

[44] The following Sabbath almost the whole town assembled to hear the message of the Lord. [45] But when the Jews saw the crowds, they were filled with jealousy and began to oppose what Paul was saying by insulting him. [46] Then Paul and Barnabas boldly said: "It was necessary that God's

message be spoken to you first. But since you reject it, and consider yourselves unworthy of eternal life, we now turn to the Gentiles!" ...
⁴⁸ When the Gentiles heard this, they rejoiced and glorified the message of the Lord, and all who had been appointed to eternal life believed. ⁴⁹ So the message of the Lord spread through the whole region. ⁵⁰ But the Jews incited the religious women of high standing and the leading men of the city. They stirred up persecution against Paul and Barnabas and expelled them from their district. ⁵¹ But shaking the dust off their feet against them, they proceeded to Iconium. ...

⁸ In Lystra a man without strength in his feet, lame from birth, and who had never walked, sat ⁹ and heard Paul speaking. After observing him closely and seeing that he had faith to be healed, ¹⁰ [Paul] said in a loud voice, "Stand up straight on your feet!" And he jumped up and started to walk around.

¹¹ When the crowds saw what Paul had done, they raised their voices, saying in the Lycaonian language, "The gods have come down to us in the form of men!" ¹² And they started to call Barnabas, Zeus, and Paul, Hermes, because he was the main speaker. ...

¹⁴ The apostles Barnabas and Paul tore their robes when they heard this and rushed into the crowd, shouting: ¹⁵ "Men! Why are you doing these things? We are men also, with the same nature as you, and we are proclaiming good news to you, that you should turn from these worthless things to the living God, who made the heaven, the earth, the sea, and everything in them." ...

¹⁹ Then some Jews came from Antioch and Iconium, and when they had won over the crowds and stoned Paul, they dragged him out of the city, thinking he was dead. ²⁰ After the disciples surrounded him, he got up and went into the town. The next day he left with Barnabas for Derbe. ...

²³ When they had appointed elders in every church and prayed with fasting, they committed them to the Lord in whom they had believed. ... ²⁶ From there they sailed back to Antioch where they had been entrusted to the grace of God for the work they had completed. ²⁷ After they arrived and gathered the church together, they reported everything God had done with them, and that He had opened the door of faith to the Gentiles.

Acts 13:1a,2-5,9a,13-16a,38-39,42-46,48-51; 14:8-12,14-15,19-20,23,26-27

God's hand is on all who are His children, and He has been with us throughout our lives. He has shaped our heritages and backgrounds. He has been weaving all sorts of experiences to shape us. He "redeems" the tragedies we've faced and even our own sinful rebelliousness to make us effective witnesses to His grace. We haven't been called to be apostles to the Gentiles, but we each have a unique destiny to discover and fulfill in the service of God.

PRINCIPLE 1

OUR LIFE EXPERIENCES UNIQUELY EQUIP US TO SERVE GOD.

God had begun to prepare the Apostle Paul for ministry as a missionary even before he was born, and this preparation continued prior to his "new birth." For a dozen or so years after his conversion, Paul went through a variety of experiences that prepared him to deal with ministry to the Gentiles, the specific ministry to which the Lord had called him. When we read in Acts 13–14 about the events of Paul's first missionary journey, we see all of this preparation and training bearing fruit in the cities of Cyprus and south central Asia Minor.

In essence, each of us who knows Christ as Savior and Lord has a unique calling and destiny regardless of our background. We may not be able to understand at the time, but God even weaves our sins and calamities into the tapestry of preparation for ministry. When Paul compared his past with that of the other apostles, he wrote, "I received mercy ... so that in me, the worst [of them], Christ Jesus might demonstrate the utmost patience as an example to those who would believe in Him for eternal life" (1 Tim. 1:16). Concerning our past failures and calamities Paul said, "He comforts us in all our affliction, so that we may be able to comfort those who are in any kind of affliction, through the comfort we ourselves receive from God" (2 Cor. 1:4).

PRINCIPLE 2

IF WE MENTOR SOMEONE WHO BECOMES MORE PROMINENT THAN WE ARE, WE WILL SHARE IN HIS ETERNAL REWARDS.

At the beginning of Acts 13, Barnabas acted as the leader of the ministry team of "Barnabas and Saul." Barnabas had championed Paul to the apostles in Jerusalem (9:27). He had recruited Paul to help him minister to the church at Antioch (11:25-26). The Holy Spirit had directed the leaders of that church to "set apart for Me Barnabas and Saul for the work that I have called them to" (13:2). When the proconsul of Cyprus wanted to hear "God's message," he "summoned Barnabas and Saul" (v. 7).

Barnabas had invested heavily in preparing Paul for ministry. He knew Paul's conversion story and how the Lord had revealed to Paul that he would have a unique ministry to the Gentiles. No doubt, he had seen evidences of the special gifts and skills Paul had for evangelizing and teaching Gentiles. Barnabas knew Paul would quickly surpass him in ministry prominence. And he did.

It happened when the sorcerer Elymas opposed the witness of "Barnabas and Saul" to the proconsul Sergius Paulus (v. 8). The Holy Spirit directed Paul to confront the sorcerer and strike him blind. Following this incident, in verse 13, Luke now refers to the ministry team as "Paul and his companions."

Barnabas willingly relinquished center stage to the man he had mentored so that he might take up the ministry to which God had called him. We need the same humility regarding the men God gives us to mentor along the path of maturity and ministry. We should rejoice over those who outstrip us in prominence. God will not forget our investment in their lives.

PRINCIPLE 3

ALL GLORY AND HONOR ULTIMATELY BELONGS TO GOD, NOT TO US.

God did marvelous works through Paul and Barnabas in the various cities of Cyprus and Asia Minor as they preached the gospel of Christ first to the Jews and then to the Gentiles. At Lystra, Paul healed a man who had been lame from birth "after observing him closely and seeing that he had faith to be healed" (14:9).

The Gentile audience exclaimed, "The gods have come down to us in the form of men!" (v. 11). They said this in the local dialect rather than in Greek, so it took Paul and Barnabas a while to realize that the priests of the temple of Zeus had started organizing worship rituals, complete with sacrifices, in their honor (v. 13).

As soon as they caught wind of what was happening, Paul and Barnabas protested vigorously that they were mere mortals with no special powers. They pointed to God as the one who had healed the lame man. They used the opportunity to call on the Gentile Lystrans to turn from idols "to the living God, who made the heaven, the earth, the sea, and everything in them" (v. 15).

We need to do more than pay lip service to the example of Paul and Barnabas. We need to use our time to honor God rather than build ourselves up. We need to invest our talents in building His kingdom more than our portfolios. We need to devote our treasures—our material possessions—to the work of God rather than our own comforts.

QUESTIONS FOR INTERACTION

1. Have there been moments in your adult life when you sensed a stronger presence of God than at other times? What was different about those times?

2. What role did other leaders in the church at Antioch play in setting the course of Paul's destiny (Acts 13:1-4)?

3. What roles might human agents play today in helping us discover God's destiny for our lives?

4. How did Paul's experience at Pisidian Antioch exemplify the experience he would have in many cities in terms of audiences, message, and reactions to the gospel (13:14-16,38-39,42-46,48-51)?

5. Why did the Gentile audience in Lystra react so differently to Paul's healing miracle than a Jewish audience would have (14:8-12)?

6. How is today's post-Christian populace becoming more like the pagan Lystrans than like the first-century Jews?

7. Why did it matter to Paul and Barnabas that the Lystrans thought them to be gods (14:14-15)? Could that have helped their mission?

8. Can you think of any ways the modern emphasis on celebrity status for Christian leaders and entertainers may tempt us to give them glory that belongs to God?

9. What explanations can you imagine for Paul's recovery from the stoning at Lystra (14:19-20)? Which explanation seems most likely? Why?

10. What things happened on Paul's first missionary journey that would have crystallized for him what his divinely appointed destiny was?

11. What are some of your experiences in ministry that have confirmed to you how God wants you to serve Him?

12. What are some of the bad things from your past that God has chosen to turn into avenues for ministry to people (2 Cor. 1:3-4)?

13. What ministry skills and gifts can you help others develop through a mentoring relationship? Whom have you helped mentor that has gone on to greater prominence than you have?

14. How do you wrestle with wanting others to recognize and appreciate you for what you do? How do you give glory to God?

CARING TIME

Even though God revealed Paul's destiny to him during his conversion experience (Acts 9:15-16), it still took him about a dozen years to be ready to fulfill it. We get so impatient to know and do immediately what God wants for each stage of our lives. God isn't trying to hide anything from us, but He doesn't get in the kind of rush we do. He often wants us to rely on people around us more than we want to. Even Paul had to rely on people like Ananias, the other disciples in Damascus, Barnabas, and the leaders of the church at Antioch to fulfill his destiny.

1. What kind of ministry are you involved in now that can help reveal God's destiny for you?

2. Who are the people you depend on for mature spiritual guidance and correction, if needed?

3. What do you sense your purpose is in the body of Christ?

4. Pray for the man to your left that God will fulfill in him the purpose He has for his life.

NEXT WEEK

Next week we will focus on the controversy that erupted in the Jerusalem church because Paul and Barnabas had established Gentile churches, and we will see how the church resolved this conflict. Jewish Christians who had lived their whole lives under the Law of Moses wrestled to understand the relationship of law and grace in the gospel of Christ. It is to their everlasting credit that they responded to God's Spirit as they did and declared salvation to be a gift of God's grace in response to faith alone.

SCRIPTURE NOTES ——————————————

ACTS 13:1A-16,38-51; 14:8--27

13:1 prophets and teachers. While the line between prophets and teachers is not that distinct, teachers were those who had a more sustained ministry of interpreting and applying Old Testament Scriptures and the words of Jesus to the life of the church. Whether or not the men mentioned here were both prophets and teachers is uncertain. It is clear Barnabas and Paul were recognized and respected as teachers (11:26).

13:3 laid hands on them. The laying on of hands was a sign of solidarity between the church and the missionaries, as well as a sign of committing them to God's grace.

13:5 Salamis. A Greek city with a substantial Jewish population. Throughout most of Paul's travels, he made it a point to begin his ministry by preaching in the synagogues in the hopes that his listeners would believe in Jesus as the Messiah (vv. 14,42; 14:1; 16:13; 17:1,10; 18:4,19; 19:8).

13:13-14 A 160-mile boat trip followed by a difficult journey over 100 miles across the Tarsus Mountains brought the missionaries to Antioch in Pisidia (not the same Antioch in 13:1). **John ... left them and went back.** No reason is given, but Paul's reaction in Acts 15:38 indicates he viewed this as some sort of failure on John (Mark's) part. **Antioch.** In the third century B.C.., the Seleucid King Nicator founded 16 cities that he called by this name in honor of his father Antiochus.

13:38 forgiveness of sins. This phrase sums up all that salvation involves. It means the believer's guilt is atoned for so that he or she enjoys a restored relationship with God, free from shame or anxiety over the past (Eph. 1:7). It also means the believer is being freed from the power of sin as his or her desires conform more and more to God's will (Rom. 6:18-19). Thirdly, it means the believer can experience a relationship of peace and intimacy with God, since all barriers to that relationship have been removed (1 Thess. 5:9-10).

13:39 everyone. Whereas in 2:39, Peter undoubtedly thought his "all" meant all Jews, Paul literally meant "everyone," Jew or Gentile. The message of the gospel of Jesus was not restricted any longer to any one group of people. **justified.** This term, borrowed from the legal system of Paul's day, was a favorite way for Paul to describe what God has done for us in Jesus (Rom. 3:24; 5:1; Gal. 3:8). In Paul's mind, this was closely tied to his view of the atonement (Lev. 16; Rom. 3:25). Because Jesus' death was a sacrifice of atonement for sin, the believer is set right before God and pronounced not guilty of sin. **from everything, which you could not be justified from through the law of Moses.** The point is not that people could actually be justified from some things by keeping the Law and only needed Christ to make up for those areas with which they had trouble, but that the Law really never served to justify anyone. In Christ, a way of being right with God is proclaimed that the Law could never give, since knowledge of the Law only made people more aware of their failure to keep it (Rom. 3:20; 8:3; Gal. 3:23-24).

13:43 *devout proselytes*. These Gentiles had fully submitted to the Jewish traditions regarding circumcision, dietary laws, and Sabbath observance.

13:48 *all who had been appointed to eternal life believed*. The fact that these Gentiles responded to the gospel with faith is the evidence that they too have been written in God's figurative book of life (Ex. 32:32; Ps. 69:28; Isa. 4:3; Dan. 12:1; Luke 10:20; Rev. 13:8; 20:12; 21:27).

13:50 *religious women of high standing*. These Gentile women respected the Jewish teachings and had ties with the synagogue.

13:51 *shaking the dust off their feet*. Typically, Jews entering Palestine from a Gentile area wiped off their feet as a symbol of cleansing themselves from any trace of Gentile contamination picked up before entering the Holy Land. Iconium. A city about 100 miles east of Pisidian Antioch.

14:8 The small Jewish community in Lystra (16:1-3) apparently did not have a synagogue. Adopting a new strategy that brought the gospel directly to the Gentiles, Paul probably preached in the Greek forum, the site of the local marketplace and gathering place for public discussion.

14:12 *Hermes ... the main speaker*. Zeus was the chief god among the Greek deities, while Hermes was the herald of the gods.

14:23 *elders*. This is the first mention of elders outside of Palestine.

14:27 *reported*. The tense of the Greek implies they "kept on reporting" what had happened. This was probably because the church was actually a combination of small house groups that met throughout the city, as at this point Christians had no common meeting places. ***opened the door of faith to the Gentiles*.** God had made a way for all Jews and Gentiles to believe. It is precisely the nature of this report that led to the conflict in chapter 15 and to the important council that was held as a result.

BREAKING THROUGH

LAST WEEK

Last week our discussion focused on the remarkable incidents surrounding Paul's first missionary journey, which he made in the company of Barnabas. We noted how God prepared Paul to reach out to the Gentiles in ways no one else could. We marveled at how graciously Barnabas stepped aside to let his protégé take center stage when the time came for the student to surpass the teacher. We also saw how quickly Paul and Barnabas gave adulation and honor to God when the pagan Lystrans tried to worship them instead.

ICEBREAKER

Some of us are rule keepers by temperament. We respect and enjoy the status quo. We quickly understand the value of traditions and the institutions that give social systems stability and coherence. Others of us automatically chafe under rules. We assume there has to be a better way of doing just about everything. We suspect that people in power are up to something, and we think it is our duty to shake up the establishment.

1. Do you tend to be a rule respecter or a boundary breaker? How did this express itself when you were in high school?

2. How does this aspect of your temperament affect the way you function in your job?

3. How does it affect the way you look at the traditions and rituals of the church?

BIBLICAL FOUNDATION

When Paul and Barnabas returned to Antioch from their first missionary journey, they immediately assembled the church and "reported everything God had done with them, and that He had opened the door of faith to the Gentiles" (Acts 14:27). This was particularly encouraging to the Christians in Antioch, since most of them were Gentiles who had come to faith in Christ. However, almost before the first blush of excitement about Gentile converts had faded from their cheeks, murmurs of disapproval rumbled through the churches of Jerusalem and Judea. These churches were made up of Jewish believers and Gentile converts to Judaism.

A Gracious Resolution

1 Some men came down from Judea and began to teach the brothers: "Unless you are circumcised according to the custom prescribed by Moses, you cannot be saved!" 2 But after Paul and Barnabas had engaged them in serious argument and debate, they arranged for Paul and Barnabas and some others of them to go up to the apostles and elders in Jerusalem concerning this controversy. 3 When they had been sent on their way by the church, they passed through both Phoenicia and Samaria, explaining in detail the conversion of the Gentiles, and they created great joy among all the brothers.

4 When they arrived at Jerusalem, they were welcomed by the church, the apostles, and the elders, and they reported all that God had done with them. 5 But some of the believers from the party of the Pharisees stood up and said, "It is necessary to circumcise them and to command them to keep the law of Moses!"

6 Then the apostles and the elders assembled to consider this matter. 7 After there had been much debate, Peter stood up and said to them: "Brothers, you are aware that in the early days God made a choice among you, that by my mouth the Gentiles would hear the gospel message and believe. 8 And God, who knows the heart, testified to them by giving the Holy Spirit, just as He also did to us. 9 He made no distinction between us and them, cleansing their hearts by faith. 10 Why, then, are you now testing God by putting on the disciples' necks a yoke that neither our forefathers nor we have been able to bear? 11 On the contrary, we believe we are saved through the grace of the Lord Jesus, in the same way they are."

12 Then the whole assembly fell silent and listened to Barnabas and Paul describing all the signs and wonders God had done through them among the Gentiles. 13 After they stopped speaking, James responded: "Brothers, listen to me! 14 Simeon has reported how God first intervened to take from the Gentiles a people for His name. 15 And the words of the prophets agree with this, as it is written:

16 After these things I will return
   and will rebuild David's tent,
      which has fallen down.
   I will rebuild its ruins
      and will set it up again,
17 so that those who are left of mankind
      may seek the Lord—

even all the Gentiles who are called
   by My name,
says the Lord who does
   these things,
[18] which have been known
   from long ago.
[19] Therefore, in my judgment, we should not cause difficulties for those
who turn to God from among the Gentiles, [20] but instead we should
write to them to abstain from things polluted by idols, from sexual immorality, from eating anything that has been strangled, and from blood.
[21] For since ancient times, Moses has had in every city those who proclaim him, and he is read aloud in the synagogues every Sabbath day."

Acts 15:1-21

PRINCIPLES TO LIVE BY

The principles that emerge from these dramatic and difficult confronta-
tions form the bedrock of Christian theology about salvation and the
church. This important controversy was between those who would exclude
people of faith who didn't keep the Old Testament Law and those who
would include them on the basis of faith alone. Without this very difficult
period of church history, Christianity would have remained a sect of Judaism. It would have deteriorated into another religion based on religiosity,
"churchianity," and so-called good works.

PRINCIPLE 1

SALVATION IS A GIFT WE RECEIVE THROUGH FAITH. A GIFT IS JUST
THAT—A "GIFT." IT IS OURS TO RECEIVE AND IT LIES BEYOND THE
LONG ARMS OF OLD TESTAMENT LAW.

Three rather distressing things happened after Paul and Barnabas returned
from their first missionary journey. First, Peter, the key leader of the
apostles, came to Antioch and hypocritically snubbed the Gentile believers to please dignitaries from the Jerusalem church (Gal. 2:12). Second,
a report arrived from the new Gentile churches in southern Asia Minor
that Jewish teachers were instructing the believers they needed to become
Jews to complete their salvation (1:6-7). Finally, Jewish teachers came to
Antioch from the Jerusalem church claiming the Gentile believers there
needed to be circumcised (Acts 15:1).

The church of Jesus Christ faced the real danger of splitting into two
warring factions—one faction believing in salvation by faith alone and another believing in the need to observe the Old Testament Law in addition
to faith in Christ. The leaders of the church at Antioch sent representatives

to Jerusalem to confer with the apostles and elders about the mind of the Lord on this issue (v. 2).

Initial debate proved fruitless, but then Peter and James spoke in succession in favor of salvation by grace through faith apart from observance of the Law of Moses (vv. 7-21). The council accepted their viewpoint, prepared a letter announcing its verdict, and sent it to the Antioch church by Paul and Barnabas and two emissaries, Judas and Silas (vv. 22-33). This announcement preserved the unity and peace of the church and affirmed the doctrine of salvation by faith.

Our actions do not give us eternal life. Only the sacrificial death of Jesus can do that. Some of the most moral people in the world are lost because they have not placed their faith in Jesus Christ to save them. In addition, once we are saved, we are secure because of God's power, not our own efforts. Once we put our faith in Jesus Christ, we are redeemed and "sealed with the promised Holy Spirit. He is the down payment of our inheritance, for the redemption of the possession, to the praise of His glory" (Eph. 1:13b-14).

PRINCIPLE 2

GODLY WORK WILL CHARACTERIZE OUR LIVES AND BE EVIDENCE OF THE INTERNAL TRANSFORMATION.

As James stands to speak he recalls the words of the Prophets. His primary point during this short address to the council suggests that there should be external evidence as testimony to an individual's internal godliness. Accordingly, there may not be any need for physical evidence such as circumcision. He concludes in saying that we should not be a hindrance to a person's transformation. Rather, we should let his life speak for itself because, after all, the "proof is in the pudding."

When the Jerusalem council affirmed that salvation was by faith in the completed work of Christ and not by observing the Law, there was never any question that grace-saved believers should lead holy lives. Believing Gentiles were people called by God's name (Acts 15:17). They were asked to respect Jewish dietary and sexual laws. Gentile believers were given no license to live selfishly.

Paul would later teach the Ephesian church: "For by grace you are saved through faith, and this is not from yourselves; it is God's gift—not from works, so that no one can boast. For we are His creation—created in Christ Jesus for good works, which God prepared ahead of time so that we should walk in them" (Eph. 2:8-10).

This does not mean that people will automatically live godly lives the moment they believe in Jesus Christ and are born again. They must be taught the will of God, especially if they are converted out of a pagan lifestyle that reflects a non-biblical value system. That is why Jesus said, "Go, therefore, and make disciples ... teaching them to observe everything I have commanded you" (Matt. 28:19-20).

PRINCIPLE 3

WE NEED TO AVOID BOTH LEGALISM AND RECKLESSNESS IN OUR CHRISTIAN LIVES. LEGALISM AND RECKLESSNESS ARE THE ENEMIES OF THE BALANCED LIFE.

It is human nature to go to extremes in almost every area of life, including politics, economics, philosophy, psychology, education, or religion. Unfortunately, this also happens in biblical Christianity. While there were Jewish Christians who wanted to turn the church into a bunch of law-keeping converts to Judaism, there were Gentiles who wanted to turn the decision by the Jerusalem Council into permission to live sinfully. The Jerusalem Council worked hard under the guidance of the Holy Spirit to produce a resolution that avoided both of these extremes.

Paul would later encourage the Galatians, "We know that no one is justified by the works of the law but by faith in Jesus Christ. And we have believed in Christ Jesus, so that we might be justified by faith in Christ and not by the works of the law, because by the works of the law no human being will be justified" (2:16). On the other hand, he would scold the Romans, "Should we continue in sin in order that grace may multiply? Absolutely not! How can we who died to sin still live in it?" (6:1-2).

One of Paul's most balanced statements about grace and holy living occurs in Titus 2:11-14. The apostle wrote, "For the grace of God has appeared, with salvation for all people, instructing us to deny godlessness and worldly lusts and to live in a sensible, righteous, and godly way in the present age, while we wait for the blessed hope and the appearing of the glory of our great God and Savior, Jesus Christ. He gave Himself for us to redeem us from all lawlessness and to cleanse for Himself a special people, eager to do good works."

QUESTIONS FOR INTERACTION

1. Which of the following statements best captures your reaction to the position of the Jewish Christians that the Gentiles needed to be circumcised? Why?
   a. They were wrong, but I can understand that they wanted to maintain the purity of God's people as taught in the Old Testament.
   b. They were wrong because they didn't trust the purifying power of the grace of God.

2. What was the position of "some of the believers from the party of the Pharisees" (Acts 15:1,5)?

3. Why did Paul and Barnabas want to go throughout Phoenicia and Samaria, reporting to the churches about their Gentile mission (v. 3)?

4. What weight would Peter's testimony have carried in this controversy (vv. 7-11)?

5. What conclusions did James, the half-brother of Jesus, draw from the testimony of Peter and from Amos 9:11-12 (Acts 15:13-19)?

6. How does James' proposal (v. 20) differ from the position of the Pharisaic believers (vv. 1,5)?

7. What evidence do you see that the church leaders were more interested in discovering the will of God than in proving their side of the controversy was right?

8. Why was it important for the apostles in Jerusalem to support the Gentile mission of Paul and Barnabas? What might have happened if Paul and Barnabas had gone on reaching Gentiles while ignoring the concerns of the Jerusalem church?

9. Why do we often have difficulty resolving conflict in our churches today?

10. What can we learn from the Jerusalem Council about resolving differences?

Going Deeper

11. How does the grace of God provide us salvation and confidence when we first believe and begin living lives of faith?

12. How do good works provide evidence of our salvation?

13. How do we find the balance between legalism and license in our beliefs and behavior?

 CARING TIME

It is hard to escape the peril of the pendulum. Jesus was certainly "full of grace and truth" (John 1:14), but we tend to swing from one to the other. Sometimes we batter people with rules in an attempt to make them conform to our opinions. We think we are defending the truth. Other times we bend over backward and ignore sin in order to make people feel good about themselves. We think we are exercising grace. It is hard to be like Jesus and be committed to grace and truth at the same time. The council at Jerusalem succeeded, and we need to try to do the same.

1. When you face disagreement, do you tend to be a controller or an appeaser?

2. How does this behavior cause you problems at home? At work? At church?

3. Go around the circle and take turns praying for one another that you can all be more committed to both grace and truth.

NEXT WEEK

Next week we will turn our attention to Paul's second missionary journey. We will see Paul and Barnabas part company over John Mark and disagree about whether or not he should be given a second chance in ministry. We will then see Paul team up with Silas to revisit the churches of Asia Minor and to launch new churches on the Greek peninsula. We will also observe Paul's growth and development as a person and as a servant of God through these exciting adventures.

SCRIPTURE NOTES

ACTS 15:1-21

15:1-4 The controversy surrounding circumcision stirred up such a debate that the church felt it necessary to call together the recognized leaders from Jerusalem and Antioch to settle the issue. This is considered to be the first Church Council.

15:3 Phoenicia. The Mediterranean coastal region north of Galilee, populated by Gentiles. Modern Lebanon. *Samaria.* The territory between Galilee and Judea, whose population was a racial mix of Gentiles and Jews from Old Testament times (2 Kings 17:24-41). Active hostility existed between first-century Jews and Samaritans.

15:5 the believers from the party of the Pharisees. The resistance at allowing Gentiles into the church originated with a small but influential sect widely respected for its adherence to the Old Testament Law and traditions. Their concern arose from a genuine desire to insure that God's honor was not violated through disregard of His Law. To them, the offer of the gospel apart from the Law was inconceivable. How could Jews possibly even share in the Lord's Supper (often connected to an actual meal) when the presence of Gentiles among them would mean defilement? The only reasonable solution these believers could see was that Gentiles needed to become Jewish. Only then could both the purity and the unity of the church be maintained.

15:7-8 As part of the discussion, Peter recounted his experience with Cornelius, which may have occurred 10 or more years earlier (10:1–11:18). The fact that Cornelius experienced the presence of the Spirit in the same way the disciples did was proof to Peter that God accepted the Gentiles quite apart from the practice of Jewish law.

15:13-21 James was a leader of the Jerusalem church, and the ultimate decision as to the position of the Jerusalem church was the leadership's decision to make. Since in Galatians 2:11-13 James appears to have represented those who believed that Gentiles could not be considered equal members of the church with Jews, it may be that this council was the turning point when he realized the scope of Jesus' mission.

15:16-18 The original context of the prophecy was the anticipation of the destruction of Israel (722 B.C.), after which God would one day return the nation to its former glory as in David's day.

15:20 write to them to abstain. These considerations sum up the laws in Leviticus 17–18 that applied to Israel and all foreigners who lived within her borders. **things polluted.** In Gentile areas meat was sold only after the animal had been sacrificed to an idol as part of a worship service. The eating of such food was later to be a source of controversy between Jewish and Gentile believers in Rome (Rom. 14:1-8) and Corinth (1 Cor. 8). **sexual immorality.** This may be related to "things polluted by idols" since idolatry sometimes involved ritual prostitution (1 Cor. 6:12-20). **anything that has been strangled, and from blood.** Jews were forbidden to eat meat that had any blood in it (Lev. 17:10-14). Gentiles would make the sharing of meals with Jewish believers easier if they would respect this tradition.

THE SECOND WIND

LAST WEEK

Last week we observed the beautiful way the Holy Spirit supernaturally guided the early church to understand and accept salvation by grace through faith alone. He guided both those who had been evangelizing the Jews for some time and those who had recently begun to evangelize the Gentiles. When controversy could have splintered the church of Jesus Christ beyond recovery, godly leaders let go of selfish interests and personal agendas in order to seek the mind of Christ and pursue it.

ICEBREAKER

We wish our relationships with family, friends, co-workers, and church peers would suddenly become perfect and stay that way for the rest of our lives. We know it isn't going to happen, but we still dream. In real life, relationships with people are hard to develop and even harder to maintain.

1. Which of these breakups has caused you the most pain? Why?
   a. Losing a girlfriend
   b. Divorce
   c. Moving
   d. Losing a job
   e. A rebellious child
   f. Retirement
   g. Other _____

2. What relationship gives you the greatest satisfaction at the moment? Why?

3. Who is the best friend you ever had who was a lot older or younger than you were? What made that friendship special?

BIBLICAL FOUNDATION

Life parades many opportunities before us every day. Each moment gives us the potential to make huge decisions. Paul's second missionary journey unfolded against a backdrop of losing some important relationships and forging new ones. We see Paul parting ways with his best friend and refusing the help of a questionable ally. We see him building a new partnership and taking on a youthful apprentice. We also see him learning from the failed relationships how to make the new ones stronger and more pleasing to God.

Going and Growing

[36] After some time had passed, Paul said to Barnabas, "Let's go back and visit the brothers in every town where we have preached the message of the Lord, and see how they're doing." [37] Barnabas wanted to take along John Mark. [38] But Paul did not think it appropriate to take along this man who had deserted them in Pamphylia and had not gone on with them to the work. [39] There was such a sharp disagreement that they parted company, and Barnabas took Mark with him and sailed off to Cyprus. [40] Then Paul chose Silas and departed, after being commended to the grace of the Lord by the brothers. [41] He traveled through Syria and Cilicia, strengthening the churches.

[1] Then he went on to Derbe and Lystra, where there was a disciple named Timothy, the son of a believing Jewish woman, but his father was a Greek. [2] The brothers at Lystra and Iconium spoke highly of him. [3] Paul wanted Timothy to go with him, so he took him and circumcised him because of the Jews who were in those places, since they all knew that his father was a Greek. [4] As they traveled through the towns, they delivered to them the decisions reached by the apostles and elders at Jerusalem. [5] So the churches were strengthened in the faith and were increased in number daily.

[6] They went through the region of Phrygia and Galatia and were prevented by the Holy Spirit from speaking the message in the province of Asia. [7] When they came to Mysia, they tried to go into Bithynia, but the Spirit of Jesus did not allow them. [8] So, bypassing Mysia, they came down to Troas. [9] During the night a vision appeared to Paul: a Macedonian man was standing and pleading with him, "Cross over to Macedonia and help us!" [10] After he had seen the vision, we immediately made efforts to set out for Macedonia, concluding that God had called us to evangelize them.

[11] Then, setting sail from Troas, we ran a straight course to Samothrace, the next day to Neapolis, [12] and from there to Philippi, a Roman colony, which is a leading city of that district of Macedonia. We stayed in that city for a number of days. ...

[1] Then they traveled through Amphipolis and Apollonia and came to Thessalonica, where there was a Jewish synagogue. [2] As usual, Paul went to them, and on three Sabbath days reasoned with them from the Scriptures, [3] explaining and showing that the Messiah had to suffer and

rise from the dead, and saying: "This is the Messiah, Jesus, whom I am proclaiming to you." [4] Then some of them were persuaded and joined Paul and Silas, including a great number of God-fearing Greeks, as well as a number of the leading women.

[5] But the Jews became jealous, and when they had brought together some scoundrels from the marketplace and formed a mob, they set the city in an uproar. ... [8] The Jews stirred up the crowd and the city officials who heard these things. [9] So taking a security bond from Jason and the others, they released them. [10] As soon as it was night, the brothers sent Paul and Silas off to Beroea.

Acts 15:36–16:12; 17:1-4,5a,8-10a

[7] Although we could have been a burden as Christ's apostles, instead we were gentle among you, as a nursing mother nurtures her own children. ... [10] You are witnesses, and so is God, of how devoutly, righteously, and blamelessly we conducted ourselves with you believers. [11] As you know, like a father with his own children, [12] we encouraged, comforted, and implored each one of you to walk worthy of God, who calls you into His own kingdom and glory.

1 Thessalonians 2:7,10-12

PRINCIPLES TO LIVE BY

Some Christians tend to evaluate their spirituality by what they know about the Bible and theology. Others tend to measure their spirituality by the quality of their behavior. God is interested in both. The incidents of Paul's second missionary journey yield some challenging principles about being committed to knowing the truth and living it out in our relationships with both believers and nonbelievers.

PRINCIPLE 1

WE MUST CONTINUE THE GROWTH PROCESS, BOTH THROUGH WHAT WE BELIEVE DOCTRINALLY AND HOW WE LIVE OUT OUR LIVES.

Whether living in Jerusalem or Antioch or traveling in Cyprus or Asia Minor, Paul and Barnabas exemplified trust, loyalty, mutual support, and oneness in heart and mind. Against this backdrop of incredible and exemplary team unity, it is rather jolting to see them face an irreconcilable disagreement. Their tempers flared, they spoke harsh words, and they separated to go in different directions (Acts 15:39).

Paul proposed returning to the churches of the first missionary journey to strengthen and encourage them (v. 36). Barnabas proposed taking John Mark along again, but Paul refused (vv. 37-38). Barnabas felt it was imperative that John Mark prove himself after his initial failure. However, Paul was not willing to risk another failure by an untrustworthy youngster. Both men were adamant—Barnabas in his concern for the man; Paul in his concern for the mission.

Both men had a point. Both men were true to their character—Barnabas as an encourager; Paul as a determined pioneer missionary. Both probably regretted that they parted in anger. Hopefully they reconciled in later days in keeping with the gospel they preached.

During the second missionary journey, Paul matured in the way he related to Christians who were struggling in their walk. This greater sensitivity likely grew out of his reflection on the conflict he had with Barnabas. Where he had been demanding and stern with John Mark, he was patient and careful in the way he brought Timothy into leadership responsibilities (1 Thess. 3:1-2; 2 Tim. 1:3-8). Where he had been confrontational and brusque when he wrote the Galatians after the first missionary trip (Gal. 3:1-3), he was gentle and nurturing when he wrote the Thessalonians during the second one (1 Thess. 2:7,11-12).

Early in his ministry, Paul focused more on doctrine and truth. However, the more he matured in his relationship with Jesus Christ, the more he matured in his relationships with others. Like Paul, we need to learn to evaluate our Christian life not only by our commitment to doctrinal truth but also by our commitment to gracious, loving relationships. In this way, we will conform more closely to the image of our Lord Jesus Christ.

PRINCIPLE 2

ALL OF US, WHETHER WE ARE TASK-DRIVEN OR PEOPLE-ORIENTED, MUST ALLOW THE HOLY SPIRIT TO CONFORM US TO THE IMAGE OF JESUS CHRIST.

The Apostle Paul appears to have been rather tough-minded by nature. Though he definitely cared about people, he could be insensitive in his relationships. He was also very task-oriented. Carrying out the Great Commission to preach the gospel to the Gentiles was always at the forefront of his mind.

Barnabas, on the other hand, appears to have been highly relational by nature. This helps explain why he intervened for Paul in Jerusalem and later stood his ground for John Mark even though he had to confront a friend in the process. He was consistently concerned for the feelings of others.

Nevertheless, Paul learned to subject his tough-mindedness to the powerful influence of the Holy Spirit. In his letter to the Galatians Paul wrote, "The fruit of the Spirit is love, joy, peace, patience, kindness, goodness, faith, gentleness, self-control" (5:22-23). Although this was primarily a confrontational epistle, it still taught that the Spirit wants to soften our hearts toward one another.

It took time for Paul to practice consistently the very truth he taught the Galatians, but it was always his goal to be like Jesus Christ. The longer Paul lived, the more the Holy Spirit tempered his natural design with the qualities of Christlikeness.

PRINCIPLE 3

GOD HAS MADE PROVISIONS TO GIVE SECOND CHANCES BOTH FOR BELIEVERS AND NONBELIEVERS ALIKE.

Thanks to Barnabas, John Mark got a second chance (Acts 15:39b). Thanks to God's grace, Paul got a second chance. Paul not only received a second chance in the way he mentored Timothy, but also through a restored, trusting relationship with John Mark (Col. 4:10; 2 Tim. 4:11). So it is with us. God wants to give all of us a second, a third, and even a fourth chance and more. That is what is meant by "grace."

This does not mean that there are no consequences, because there certainly are. Every time we fail, we reap what we sow. The consequences, of course, are determined by the seriousness of our sin. However, God does not want us to wallow in the past. He wants us to experience forgiveness, forget past failures, and press on. We serve a God who can take our mistakes and failures and cause them to work together for good (Rom. 8:28).

QUESTIONS FOR INTERACTION

1. Do you think it is harder for a task-oriented man to become more people-focused or for a people-oriented man to become more task-focused? Why?

2. Why did Barnabas want to take Mark on the second missionary trip (Acts 15:37)? Why didn't Paul want to take him (v. 38)?

3. What were the strengths and weaknesses of Barnabas' case for and Paul's case against Mark?

4. What do you think Paul needed from his new relationship with Silas (v. 40)? Why would he select another young protégé, Timothy, to replace Mark (16:1-3)?

5. What would it have meant to Paul's ministry to have such clear direction from the Holy Spirit about going to Macedonia (vv. 6-10)?

6. When have you felt very confident about a decision or action because of the leading of God's Spirit?

7. What was Paul's experience in the Greek city of Thessalonica (17:1-4)?

8. What emotions did Paul in fact feel for the Thessalonians (1 Thess. 2:7-12)?

9. What evidence suggests that Paul was becoming more sensitive to people as he matured in Christ?

10. Do you need to become more people-sensitive or more task-oriented in order to be a balanced disciple? How is God working on you to achieve this?

GOING DEEPER

11. Do you tend to evaluate your spiritual life by what you know about the Bible or by how you treat people? How can you achieve better balance between these?

12. How did Mark get a second chance to make up for deserting Paul and Barnabas? How did Paul get a second chance to make up for being so harsh on Mark?

13. "God wants to give all of us a second, a third, and even a fourth chance and more. That is what is meant by 'grace.'" How do you feel about this statement?

CARING TIME

We don't know how long it took Paul to repair his relationships with Barnabas and Mark. We have no idea what words and actions it took. We do know how Barnabas valued people, and we know that Paul often addressed the issue of reconciliation in his writing (Rom. 12:9-21; Eph. 4:25-27, 31-32). We should take this opportunity to encourage one another and to repair any of our strained or damaged relationships.

1. What signs of neglect or damage should you deal with in your relationship with your wife?

2. What signs of neglect or damage should you deal with in your relationships with your children?

3. How can we hold one another accountable to work on these relationships throughout the balance of this group study?

NEXT WEEK

Next week we will look at Paul's third missionary journey and focus our attention on his relationship with the elders of the church at Ephesus. In his ministry to those spiritual leaders, we will see what Paul learned about the heart of a shepherd for the flock of God through decades of ministry to the Gentiles. Ephesus was the chief city of Asia Minor, and the Ephesian church took the lead in evangelizing cities all around it. Paul needed to be sure that the leaders of this church reflected the heart of the Good Shepherd, Jesus Christ.

SCRIPTURE NOTES

ACTS 15:36–16:12; 17:1-4,5A,8-10A

15:38 who had deserted them. While the word used to describe Mark's leaving in 13:13 is a neutral one that implies nothing negative, the word used here is related to apostasy. Luke does not tell us why Mark left, but Paul certainly viewed it as a serious defect and was unwilling to let him try again.

15:39-40 a sharp disagreement. Barnabas' concern may have been motivated in part by the fact that Mark was his cousin (Col. 4:10), but it is characteristic of Barnabas. Years before it had been he who insisted that Paul be given a chance to prove himself to the apostles (9:27) and who recognized Paul's calling (11:25-26). On the other hand, Paul was concerned about the immediate needs and demands of such a rigorous journey. Undoubtedly, Mark's earlier departure had placed increased demands on Paul and Barnabas, and he was unwilling to risk that again. While the ongoing action focuses on Paul and Silas, Barnabas and Mark also left Antioch on a missionary trip as they returned to Cyprus (13:4-12).

15:41–16:5 Whereas the limits of Paul's first journey had been achieved by a sea voyage to Cyprus and southern Asia Minor and an overland trek eastward from Perga in Pamphylia to the border of Cilicia, this time Paul went west from Antioch in Syria, going overland through the provinces until he reached Derbe (v. 1; 14:20).

16:1-3 As the son of a Jewish woman. Jewish law said Timothy ought to have been circumcised as an infant. Perhaps his Gentile father (who may have been dead at the time of Paul's visit) had forbidden it. At any rate, for Paul to allow Timothy, a Jew, to accompany him apart from following the age-old Jewish custom of circumcision would have communicated to other Jews that he had no regard whatsoever for their honored traditions.

16:6-7 the Holy Spirit ... the Spirit of Jesus. Luke clearly identified the ongoing work of Jesus with the agency of the Holy Spirit in the lives of the apostles. ***did not allow them.*** Why Jesus would not allow Paul, Silas, and Timothy to preach in Asia and Bithynia is not given. Later on, the apostle Peter was in contact with churches in that area, so they were not left bereft of the gospel (1 Pet. 1:1).

16:8 down to Troas. An important seaport on the Aegean Sea. While it appears Paul did not do any evangelistic work at this time, he did later on (2 Cor. 2:12).

16:9 Macedonia. This area of northern Greece had been the dominant power under Alexander the Great in the fourth century B.C.

17:5 In Philippi, economic interest motivated the opposition to Paul and Silas. In Thessalonica, it was the jealousy of the Jews who may have envied Paul's success in converting Gentiles that had for so long resisted Jewish attempts at proselytizing.

17:9 a security bond from Jason and the others. Since Paul himself could not be brought before the officials, they simply insisted that Jason post a bond, assuring them that he would no longer be a host to Paul so that he would have to leave the city.

1 THESSALONIANS 2:7,10-12

2:7 gentle ... as a nursing mother. Paul was not hesitant to use this female imagery for himself, as he described his love for his spiritual children.

2:11 like a father with his own children. In some respects, Paul was what a single parent must be—both mother (v. 7) and father! In the ancient world, the father's role was to see that his children learned how to live as responsible citizens.

ORIENTATION

LAST WEEK

Last week we looked at Paul's second missionary journey. We focused on the relational breakdown that immediately preceded the journey and the growth in the relationships that seemed to characterize Paul during his travels and ministry with Silas and Timothy. We explored our own personality types and the need to rely on the Holy Spirit to conform our relational styles to that of Jesus.

ICEBREAKER

Paul's final words to the elders of the Ephesian church contained challenges to be good shepherds of God's flock. People in the first century knew a lot about caring for sheep. Most twenty-first century men experience sheep when they take their children to the petting zoo. Sheep are high-maintenance, low-intelligence, social creatures that need constant attention and vigilant protection. In the Bible, the phrase "sheep without a shepherd" describes people in a hopeless situation (Num. 27:17; 1 Kings 22:17; Ezek. 34:5-6; Zech. 10:2; Mark 6:34).

1. What pets did you have as a child? What were your responsibilities in caring for them?

2. What pets have you had as an adult? What have you learned about people from caring for animals?

3. What kinds of bad things can happen to "sheep without a shepherd" out on the open range?

BIBLICAL FOUNDATION

When Jesus chose a metaphor to describe and illustrate His concern and love for people, He identified Himself as the Good Shepherd (John 10:11a). He not only knew His sheep but was willing to die for them (vv. 11b,15b). He was—and is—the perfect pastor.

Paul modeled his own ministry style after that of Jesus Christ. In fact, he eventually paid the ultimate price, just as the Savior did. By his third missionary journey, Paul, who had begun his ministry as a zealous, tough-minded ex-Pharisee, had become a caring, gentle shepherd through the transforming work of the Holy Spirit.

Of Shepherds and Wolves

[1] While Apollos was in Corinth, Paul traveled through the interior regions and came to Ephesus. ...

[8] Then he entered the synagogue and spoke boldly over a period of three months, engaging in discussion and trying to persuade them about the things related to the kingdom of God. [9] But when some became hardened and would not believe, slandering the Way in front of the crowd, he withdrew from them and met separately with the disciples, conducting discussions every day in the lecture hall of Tyrannus. [10] And this went on for two years, so that all the inhabitants of the province of Asia, both Jews and Greeks, heard the word of the Lord.

[11] God was performing extraordinary miracles by Paul's hands, [12] so that even facecloths or work aprons that had touched his skin were brought to the sick, and the diseases left them, and the evil spirits came out of them.

[13] Then some of the itinerant Jewish exorcists attempted to pronounce the name of the Lord Jesus over those who had evil spirits, saying, "I command you by the Jesus whom Paul preaches!" [14] Seven sons of Sceva, a Jewish chief priest, were doing this. [15] The evil spirit answered them, "Jesus I know, and Paul I recognize—but who are you?" [16] Then the man who had the evil spirit leaped on them, overpowered them all, and prevailed against them, so that they ran out of that house naked and wounded. [17] This became known to everyone who lived in Ephesus, both Jews and Greeks. Then fear fell on all of them, and the name of the Lord Jesus was magnified. [18] And many who had become believers came confessing and disclosing their practices, [19] while many of those who had practiced magic collected their books and burned them in front of everyone. So they calculated their value, and found it to be 50,000 pieces of silver. [20] In this way the Lord's message flourished and prevailed. ...

[23] During that time there was a major disturbance about the Way. ... [29] So the city was filled with confusion; and they rushed all together into the amphitheater, dragging along Gaius and Aristarchus, Macedonians who were Paul's traveling companions. [30] Though Paul wanted to go in before the people, the disciples did not let him. [31] Even some of the provincial officials of Asia, who were his friends, sent word to him, pleading with him not to take a chance by going into the amphitheater. ...

1 After the uproar was over, Paul sent for the disciples, encouraged them, and after saying good-bye, departed to go to Macedonia. [2] And when he had passed through those areas and exhorted them at length, he

came to Greece [3] and stayed three months. When he was about to set sail for Syria, a plot was devised against him by the Jews, so a decision was made to go back through Macedonia. ...

[16] Paul had decided to sail past Ephesus so he would not have to spend time in the province of Asia, because he was hurrying to be in Jerusalem, if possible, for the day of Pentecost. [17] Now from Miletus, he sent to Ephesus and called for the elders of the church. [18] And when they came to him, he said to them: "You know, from the first day I set foot in Asia, how I was with you the whole time— [19] serving the Lord with all humility, with tears, and with the trials that came to me through the plots of the Jews— [20] and that I did not shrink back from proclaiming to you anything that was profitable, or from teaching it to you in public and from house to house. [21] I testified to both Jews and Greeks about repentance toward God and faith in our Lord Jesus. ...

[25] "And now I know that none of you, among whom I went about preaching the kingdom, will ever see my face again. [26] Therefore I testify to you this day that I am innocent of everyone's blood, [27] for I did not shrink back from declaring to you the whole plan of God. [28] Be on guard for yourselves and for all the flock, among whom the Holy Spirit has appointed you as overseers, to shepherd the church of God, which He purchased with His own blood. [29] I know that after my departure savage wolves will come in among you, not sparing the flock. [30] And men from among yourselves will rise up with deviant doctrines to lure the disciples into following them. [31] Therefore be on the alert, remembering that night and day for three years I did not stop warning each one of you with tears.

[32] "And now I commit you to God and to the message of His grace, which is able to build you up and to give you an inheritance among all who are sanctified. [33] I have not coveted anyone's silver or gold or clothing. [34] You yourselves know that these hands have provided for my needs, and for those who were with me. [35] In every way I've shown you that by laboring like this, it is necessary to help the weak and to keep in mind the words of the Lord Jesus, for He said, 'It is more blessed to give than to receive.' "

Acts 19:1a,8-20,23,29-31; 20:1-3,16-21,25-35

PRINCIPLES TO LIVE BY

Shepherds often spent long periods of time alone with the flock in the wilderness. Establishing "direction," as it were, was a priority as direction was relevant to home, food, and shelter. It was very important for a shepherd to know his surroundings and be able to sense and steer away from danger. Paul's passion for discipling and shepherding believers continued to grow on his third missionary journey. With the passage of time, he saw how quickly false teachers could lead his new converts astray. Consequently, Paul increased his efforts to minister to these people at a much more personal level.

Paul's shepherding heart shows itself best during his three-year ministry in Ephesus. Ephesus was the major city of the Roman province of Asia. Paul had stopped here briefly on his second missionary journey (Acts 18:19-20), and he had promised to return if God so willed (v. 21). What God had in mind for Paul in Ephesus was his longest ministry in any city he visited during his distinguished ministry to the Gentiles. Because of that teaching, discipling, and shepherding ministry, cities all around Ephesus would hear and respond to the gospel of Christ.

Paul's shepherding model touches all of us, whether we are pastors, fathers, employers, or neighborss. There are two major principles we can draw from Paul's interaction with the elders at the church of Ephesus.

PRINCIPLE 1

EFFECTIVE CATALYSTS MODEL GOD'S TRUTH FOR EVERYONE WITHIN THEIR CIRCLES.

When Paul returned to Ephesus, he spent three months reasoning with the Jewish population in their synagogue (Acts 19:8). When opposition made that approach unproductive, Paul rented a lecture hall from a man named Tyrannus. There he "met separately with the disciples, conducting discussions every day" (v. 9). This developed into a different outreach strategy for Paul. Rather than going to people in their daily settings, people from all over Ephesus and the surrounding territory started coming to his daily teaching sessions.

Over the next two years "all the inhabitants of the province of Asia, both Jews and Greeks, heard the word of the Lord" (v. 10). Many became believers, returned to their own cities, and started churches, probably in Smyrna, Pergamum, Thyatira, Sardis, Philadelphia, Laodicea, Colosse, and Hierapolis (Rev. 1:11; Col. 4:13). By the end of his extended stay in Ephesus, Paul knew the leaders of the Ephesian church and all its satellite churches more personally than he knew those of any other church he had founded.

Paul eventually left Ephesus to visit the Greek churches and collect their offering for the poor saints in Jerusalem. He headed for Palestine from Greece with some sense of urgency, "hurrying to be in Jerusalem, if possible, for the day of Pentecost" (Acts 20:16). He didn't want to stop at Ephesus because he knew such a visit would take a long time. Instead, he summoned the Ephesian elders to meet him at the nearby port city of Miletus (v. 17). There Paul shared with these elders his final thoughts about how to lead God's people.

In a nutshell, Paul told them to set an example of how they wanted their people to live. His words to them parallel these two verses from his epistles: "Be imitators of me, as I also am of Christ" (1 Cor. 11:1) and "You are witnesses, and so is God, of how devoutly, righteously, and blamelessly we conducted ourselves with you believers" (1 Thess. 2:10).

This modeling principle is particularly applicable to those of us who are fathers. The only way young children comprehend what the invisible, heavenly Father is like is to see God in us, their visible, earthly fathers.

PRINCIPLE 2

MATURE CHRISTIAN MEN MUST REFLECT THE QUALITIES OF GOOD SHEPHERDS.

The world today—as much if not more than at any other time—requires leaders with the ability to thrive, lead, and remain standing in a hostile environment. Ephesus was a pagan city permeated with occultism. Paul's ministry there carried a constant flavor of spiritual warfare against dark forces. The sons of Sceva tried to imitate Paul's power as an exorcist by calling on the name of Jesus (Acts 19:13-16). Converts burned occult writing and paraphernalia valued at 50,000 pieces of silver (vv. 18-20). Worshipers of the goddess Artemis, the special deity of Ephesus, sparked a riot meant to destroy the Christian movement (vv. 21-41).

It is no wonder Paul wrote the Ephesians: "For our battle is not against flesh and blood, but against the rulers, against the authorities, against the world powers of this darkness, against the spiritual forces of evil in the heavens. This is why you must take up the full armor of God, so that you may be able to resist in the evil day, and having prepared everything, to take your stand" (Eph. 6:12-13).

Obviously, the elders of the Ephesian church needed to be mature men of God to lead in such a spiritually hostile environment. Paul had modeled for them **unselfish and compassionate leadership**: "serving the Lord with all humility, ... remembering that night and day for three years I did not stop warning each one of you with tears" (Acts 20:19a,31b). At the same time, he had set an example of **bold and uncompromising leadership.** "I did not shrink back from proclaiming to you anything that was profitable .... I did not shrink back from declaring to you the whole plan of God" (vv. 20,27).

The Ephesian church included Jews and Gentiles. Paul had exemplified **fair and impartial leadership**. "I testified to both Jews and Greeks about repentance toward God and faith in our Lord Jesus" (v. 21). He had mentored the Ephesian elders to provide **sacrificial and dedicated leadership.** "I count my life of no value to myself, so that I may finish my course and the ministry I received from the Lord Jesus, to testify to the gospel of God's grace" (v. 24).

Paul knew that leaders are subject to attacks from spiritual powers and inner weaknesses. To protect against the former, he advocated **accountable and pastoral leadership.** "Be on guard for yourselves and for all the flock, among whom the Holy Spirit has appointed you as overseers, to shepherd the church of God, which He purchased with His own blood" (v. 28). No pastoral leader dare operate apart from the protection that accountability to others provides. To protect against inner weaknesses, Paul modeled **unselfish and generous leadership.** "I have not coveted anyone's silver or gold or clothing. ... It is necessary to help the weak and to keep in mind the words of the Lord Jesus, for He said, 'It is more blessed to give than to receive' " (vv. 33,35b).

These qualities should be the goal of all believers. They are what make a man a good husband, a good father, a good employer or employee, and a good neighbor—not just a good pastor with a shepherd's heart.

QUESTIONS FOR INTERACTION

1. Who are the best examples in your life for each of these roles?
   a. A good employer or employee
   b. A good husband
   c. A good father
   d. A good Christ-follower
   e. A good friend

2. What was the spiritual climate of the Ephesian Jewish community at this time (Acts 19:8-9,13-17)?

3. What was the spiritual climate of the Gentile population in Ephesus at this time (vv. 9-12,17-20,23,29-31)?

4. Why do you think God chose to demonstrate His power so mightily in Ephesus (vv. 11-12)?

5. What evidences do you see that the Ephesian believers were earnest about their faith in Christ?

6. When Paul reviewed his Ephesian ministry, what things stood out to him as noteworthy (20:18-21,25-26)?

7. What challenges to be good shepherds did Paul give to the Ephesian elders (vv. 27-31)?

8. What fundamental message did Paul save for his parting exhortation to the Ephesian elders (vv. 33-35)?

9. In what ways is the spiritual climate of your community similar to that of first-century Ephesus?

10. Which idea that Paul shared with the Ephesian elders do you most need to put into practice to become a more effective leader?

Going Deeper

11. Paul wrote the Corinthians: "Be imitators of me, as I also am of Christ" (1 Cor. 11:1). How can you model the character of Christ in your employment?

12. How can you model the character of Christ to your neighbors?

13. The qualities required of pastors "should be the goal of all believers." How do you react to the notion that God expects the same qualities of you?

Caring Time

Perhaps the hardest place for a man to be a good shepherd is within his family. For some reason, we all struggle to be humble, thorough, impartial, sacrificial, and generous servants to the people we love the most.

1. How would your wife like you to be a better shepherd to her?

2. How would your children like you to be a better shepherd to them?

3. How has being part of this men's group prepared you to be a better shepherd to your family? How can we help you more in the future?

Next Week

Next week we will survey Paul's trip to Jerusalem, the riot that broke out around him at the temple, his arrest, and his imprisonments in Jerusalem and Caesarea. We will read the defenses he made to the Jerusalem mob, to the governors Felix and Festus, and to King Agrippa. This lengthy portion of Scripture (Acts 21–26) illustrates that obedience to the Word and to the Spirit may lead us along paths of suffering and pain. Even when our friends try to spare us that pain, we need to remain true to God's will.

Scripture Notes

Acts 19:1A,8-20,23,29-31; 20:1-3,16-21,25-35

19:8-20 Ephesus became the hub of Paul's ministry for three years (20:31), two of which were spent speaking in a lecture hall (19:9-10). During this time, churches were founded in Colosse, Hierapolis, and the other six cities mentioned in Revelation 1:11. It was also here that Paul wrote 1 Corinthians.

19:9 lecture hall of Tyrannus. Either the lecture hall of a local philosopher or a hall rented out to traveling philosophers by a businessman. Tyrannus meant "Tyrant." If he was a philosopher, his students may have given him this name.

19:10 province of Asia. The province of Asia was the political division of the Roman Empire that occupied the western end of Asia Minor. The cities of this province were Greek (Hellenistic) in culture.

19:11 extraordinary miracles. See the similar miracles wrought by Peter in 5:15-16. Ephesus was a city renowned for its magic arts. For that reason, this type of evidence was necessary to convince people that the power of the gospel was greater than that of magic.

19:13 itinerant Jewish exorcists. Jesus frequently cast out demons as evidence of His divine power. He also alluded to the practice of exorcism among the Pharisees in Judea (Matt. 12:27). In Ephesus, exorcism within Judaism seems to have been colored by the occult practices that pervaded popular culture. These traveling exorcists tried to use the name of Jesus as an incantation and suffered the consequences of their blasphemy.

19:14 Sceva. There was never a high priest in Jerusalem by that name, although he may have been a member of the high priest's family. He was probably an unusually successful exorcist who assumed the title for himself to command more respect (and business) from people in the area.

19:18 *many who had become believers*. The tense of the word implies that these Christians still secretly practiced magic arts. The incident with Sceva's sons showed them they needed to lay aside these practices once for all.

19:19 *value ... 50,000 pieces of silver*. An incredible amount when one considers "a piece of silver" equaled a day's wages!

19:29 *Gaius and Aristarchus, Macedonians*. Gaius and Aristarchus were traveling companions and partners in ministry with Paul. Only Aristarchus was a Macedonian from Thessalonica (20:4; 27:2). Gaius was from Derbe in Galatia (20:4).

20:25 *none of you ... will ever see my face again*. A few weeks earlier, Paul had written to the Romans that after he went to Jerusalem he hoped to visit them and proceed to Spain since his work in Macedonia and Achaia (and presumably Asia) was accomplished (Rom. 15:23-24). Whether this is why he said he would not see these people again or he subsequently felt that the warnings of the Spirit (Acts 20:23) were to prepare him for death is uncertain.

20:35 *more blessed to give*. This saying of Jesus does not appear in Matthew, Mark, Luke, or John. It is likely Paul heard many sayings of Jesus that aren't in the Gospels but which had been circulated by the other apostles and Galilean disciples who had known the Lord.

A MAN OF CONVICTION

LAST WEEK

Last week we looked at the three-year ministry at Ephesus that occupied a significant portion of Paul's third missionary journey. We paid particular attention to Paul's final challenge to the elders of this church that he knew so well and loved so dearly. He urged them to be good shepherds who would selflessly serve and protect the church with no thought for personal gain or glory. We considered how these same qualities make us better husbands, fathers, neighbors, and employers or employees.

ICEBREAKER

We will see in Acts 21–26 the many trials that Paul experienced—a riot in which the mob beat him, an arrest and threatened flogging, an open-ended imprisonment on false charges, and the constant risk of being handed over to enemies who wanted to kill him. Through it all, he never lost sight of his desire to share the gospel in Rome (19:21; Rom. 15:24,28).

1. What is the closest you've come to being caught up in an out-of-control mob? How did you feel?

2. What is the most serious encounter you've had with the police? How did it make you feel?

3. Which of these adventures would you like to experience but have never had the opportunity?
   a. Skydiving
   b. Rafting the Colorado River
   c. Hiking the Appalachian Trail
   d. Bungee jumping
   e. Climbing Mt. McKinley
   f. Spelunking
   g. Other _____

Paul was charged with delivering the church's collection to those most in need in Jerusalem. As he initiated his journey he received several warnings about the dangers that awaited him in the Holy City. At the same time, he sensed a strong compulsion from the Lord that he needed to make this trip. Many of Paul's friends thought the warnings meant that God didn't want him to go. Paul realized that these "mixed messages" were not contradictory, but complementary. The primary message was "Go;" the qualifying message was "Be ready for great adversity."

Paul's Broken Eggs Made God's Omelet

[10] While we were staying there many days, a prophet named Agabus came down from Judea. [11] He came to us, took Paul's belt, tied his own feet and hands, and said, "This is what the Holy Spirit says: 'In this way the Jews in Jerusalem will bind the man who owns this belt, and deliver him into Gentile hands.' " [12] When we heard this, both we and the local people begged him not to go up to Jerusalem.

[13] Then Paul replied, "What are you doing, weeping and breaking my heart? For I am ready not only to be bound, but also to die in Jerusalem for the name of the Lord Jesus."

[14] Since he would not be persuaded, we stopped talking and simply said, "The Lord's will be done!"

[15] After these days we got ready and went up to Jerusalem. ...

[27] Jews from the province of Asia saw [Paul] in the temple complex, stirred up the whole crowd, and seized him, [28] shouting, "Men of Israel, help! This is the man who teaches everyone everywhere against our people, our law, and this place. What's more, he also brought Greeks into the temple and has profaned this holy place." [29] For they had previously seen Trophimus the Ephesian in the city with him, and they supposed that Paul had brought him into the temple complex.

[30] The whole city was stirred up, and the people rushed together. They seized Paul, dragged him out of the temple complex, and at once the gates were shut. ...

[23] As they were yelling and flinging aside their robes and throwing dust into the air, [24] the commander ordered him to be brought into the barracks ...

[12] When it was day, the Jews formed a conspiracy and bound themselves under a curse: neither to eat nor to drink until they had killed Paul. [13] There were more than 40 who had formed this plot. ...

[23] [The commander] summoned two of his centurions and said, "Get 200 soldiers ready with 70 cavalry and 200 spearmen to go to Caesarea at nine tonight. [24] Also provide mounts so they can put Paul on them

and bring him safely to Felix the governor." ...

1 After five days Ananias the high priest came down with some elders and a lawyer named Tertullus. These men presented their case against Paul to the governor. ...

22 Since Felix was accurately informed about the Way, he adjourned the hearing, saying, "When Lysias the commander comes down, I will decide your case." 23 He ordered that the centurion keep Paul under guard, though he could have some freedom, and that he should not prevent any of his friends from serving him. ...

26 At the same time he was also hoping that money would be given to him by Paul. For this reason he sent for him quite often and conversed with him.

27 After two years had passed, Felix received a successor, Porcius Festus, and because he wished to do a favor for the Jews, Felix left Paul in prison.

1 Three days after Festus arrived in the province, he went up to Jerusalem from Caesarea. 2 Then the chief priests and the leaders of the Jews presented their case against Paul to him; and they appealed, 3 asking him to do them a favor against Paul, that he might summon him to Jerusalem. They were preparing an ambush along the road to kill him. ...

9 Then Festus, wanting to do a favor for the Jews, replied to Paul, "Are you willing to go up to Jerusalem, there to be tried before me on these charges?"

10 But Paul said: "I am standing at Caesar's tribunal, where I ought to be tried. I have done no wrong to the Jews, as even you can see very well. ...

13 After some days had passed, King Agrippa and Bernice arrived in Caesarea and paid a courtesy call on Festus. 14 Since they stayed there many days, Festus presented Paul's case to the king, saying, "There's a man who was left as a prisoner by Felix." ...

22 Then Agrippa said to Festus, "I would like to hear the man myself." "Tomorrow," he said, "you will hear him." ...

1 Agrippa said to Paul, "It is permitted for you to speak for yourself." Then Paul stretched out his hand and began his defense: 2 "I consider myself fortunate, King Agrippa, that today I am going to make a defense before you about everything I am accused of by the Jews, 3 especially since you are an expert in all the Jewish customs and controversies. ...

19 "King Agrippa, I was not disobedient to the heavenly vision. 20 Instead, I preached to those in Damascus first, and to those in Jerusalem and in all the region of Judea, and to the Gentiles, that they should repent and turn to God, and do works worthy of repentance. 21 For this reason the Jews seized me in the temple complex and were trying to kill me. 22 Since I have obtained help that comes from God, to this day I stand and testify to both small and great, saying nothing else than what

the prophets and Moses said would take place— ²³ that the Messiah must suffer, and that as the first to rise from the dead, He would proclaim light to our people and to the Gentiles."

²⁴ As he was making his defense this way, Festus exclaimed in a loud voice, "You're out of your mind, Paul! Too much study is driving you mad!"

²⁵ But Paul replied, "I'm not out of my mind, most excellent Festus. On the contrary, I'm speaking words of truth and good judgment. ²⁶ For the king knows about these matters. It is to him I am actually speaking boldly. For I'm not convinced that any of these things escapes his notice, since this was not done in a corner! ²⁷ King Agrippa, do you believe the prophets? I know you believe."

²⁸ Then Agrippa said to Paul, "Are you going to persuade me to become a Christian so easily?"

²⁹ "I wish before God," replied Paul, "that whether easily or with difficulty, not only you but all who listen to me today might become as I am—except for these chains."

Acts 21:10-15,27b-30; 22:23-24a; 23:12-13,23-24; 24:1,22-23,26-27;
25:1-3,9-10,13-14,22; 26:1-3a, 19-29

Principles to Live By

We tend to assume that when we are living in the center of God's will, life's circumstances will flow tranquilly around us and we will experience peace and harmony. Fortunately, that is often true. There are occasions, however, when it isn't. In some of the key transitional moments of our lives, we may have to face turmoil, uncertainty, opposition, and real emotional (if not physical) distress.

Principle 1

LIVING IN GOD'S GOOD, PLEASING, AND PERFECT WILL DOES NOT EXEMPT US FROM PHYSICAL PAIN, EMOTIONAL STRUGGLES, AND SPIRITUAL BATTLES.

Paul's decision to go to Jerusalem was definitely God's perfect will for him, but the results were anything but pleasant. He almost lost his life. He experienced excruciating physical pain, nearly unbearable emotional agony, and intense spiritual struggles against Satan himself.

All this arose out of a charitable mission to deliver a collection from the churches of Greece and Asia Minor to the needy saints in Jerusalem. Representatives of several of the churches accompanied Paul to deliver the money. One of them was Trophimus from Ephesus (Acts 20:4). His presence with Paul in Jerusalem (21:29) prompted visiting Ephesian Jews to accuse Paul publicly of taking a Gentile into forbidden temple precincts. This charge triggered the riot that set in motion more than two years of imprisonment for Paul in Caesarea (24:27), while various Roman officials wrangled with the Jewish Sanhedrin about what to do with him.

There are Christian leaders today who teach that God's will for His children involves material prosperity, all the trappings of "the good life," and freedom from illness. If this were true, why did the apostles suffer and die without any of these things? Why did many New Testament believers face persecution? Why do many Christians around the world today face poverty, suffering, and persecution? Because, as Paul wrote Timothy, "All those who want to live a godly life in Christ Jesus will be persecuted" (2 Tim. 3:12).

Fortunately, most of us have never faced physical persecution just because we are Christians. In fact, God's will generally is that we be able to "lead a tranquil and quiet life in all godliness and dignity" (1 Tim. 2:2). However, this is no guarantee we will not suffer persecution.

In addition, physical and emotional tragedies happen in this world because of the overall effect of sin. Being a Christian and living in God's will does not exempt us from the lingering effects of Adam's failure in the garden of Eden.

The good news is not that God exempts us from suffering. The good news is that He goes through our sufferings with us and makes "all things work together for the good of those who love God: those who are called according to His purpose" (Rom. 8:28).

PRINCIPLE 2

IT IS IN LIFE'S CRISES THAT WE CAN DEMONSTRATE OUR CHARACTER AND WITNESS MOST POWERFULLY FOR JESUS CHRIST.

Paul faced several life crises when he brought the gift to Jerusalem from the Gentile churches of Greece and Asia Minor. The mob at the temple took him out of the holy compound so they could kill him (Acts 21:30-31). Although Roman soldiers rescued Paul, the crowd must have seriously mauled him before they arrived. The Romans threatened him with flogging (22:24). Jewish extremists plotted to assassinate him (23:12-14).

After being whisked away to safety in Caesarea, Paul languished in prison for two years (24:27). During that time, the Jewish authorities tried periodically to get the Romans to turn him over to them for execution. Felix, the governor, kept hinting to Paul that he could be bribed into releasing him (v. 26). Festus, the next governor, appeared inclined to turn him over to the Jews, so Paul felt compelled to appeal to the imperial court in Rome (25:9-10). That may sound like a convenient way to get to Rome—at government expense even—but Paul had no way of knowing what dangers lurked in the justice Nero might dispense.

However, Paul was ready to suffer for Christ's sake. Such suffering seemed purposeful to him. Festus and King Agrippa thought Paul fanatical in his commitment to Christ (26:24,28). They could not grasp his sense of purpose.

For the most part, it is not as difficult to maintain our character and witness during times of prosperity and good fortune. We will all be given an opportunity, however, to develop our character through crisis and adversity. How we handle it can give us a powerful testimony for Christ.

QUESTIONS FOR INTERACTION

1. In what kind of stressful situation(s) do you find yourself trying to trust God to work out His will in your life?
   a. A fractured marriage
   b. Bad health
   c. An employment issue
   d. Parent-child conflict
   e. Struggle with an addiction
   f. Other _____

2. Why did Paul's friends try to talk him out of going to Jerusalem?

3. When should we appreciate but politely refuse the advice of well-meaning friends?

4. What do you suppose Paul reminded himself of during his lengthy imprisonment, in order to keep from losing heart?

5. What do you need to remind yourself of during stressful situations in order to keep from being discouraged?

6. What did each of the following want from Paul during his imprisonment?
   a. The Jewish establishment
   b. Felix, the first governor
   c. Porcius Festus, the second governor
   d. King Agrippa
   e. God

7. What do you think God wants to accomplish in your life through the stressful situation(s) you are facing?

8. What was Paul's desire for all the people who imprisoned and mistreated him?

9. What are your desires for the people who are causing stress in your life? How does your attitude toward these difficult people compare with Paul's attitude toward those who persecuted him?

10. How can you pray for those who cause you stress? How can you exemplify or verbalize Christ's love for them?

GOING DEEPER

11. Why might some preachers avoid teaching about difficulty and adversity?

12. To what extent do each of the following contribute in bringing suffering to our lives?
    a. The results of the fall of Adam
    b. Opposition from the world and the Devil
    c. Our own moral failings and foolish choices

13. How can we begin to discern the possible purposes of our suffering?

CARING TIME

Difficult circumstances trigger stress, but in the final analysis, stress is our internal reaction to difficulties. Some people, like the Apostle Paul, handle calamities and disasters without red lining their stress meters. Others max out their stress meters at something as slight as a frown. We probably all want to be more calm like Paul and less stressed out.

1. What are the most common causes of stress in your life?

2. How do you react to these stress-producing situations?

3. How can talking about these stress producers and praying about them with others reduce your stress level?

Next Week

As we conclude our study next week about the life of the Apostle Paul, we will see that he finished his ministry with the same enthusiasm and drive with which he began it. He reached Rome. He shared the gospel of Christ there with important people and common people. He wrote several of his epistles in the final stages of his career. He finished his race well. That is a worthwhile goal for each of us.

Scripture Notes

Acts 21:10-15,27-30; 22:23-24a; 23:12-13,23-24; 24:1,22-27; 25:1-3,9-14,22; 26:1-3a,19-29

21:11 Agabus enacted his prophecy to accent its impact. Enacted prophecies were sometimes done by the Old Testament prophets as well (1 Kings 11:29-39, Ezek. 4). **Paul's belt**. A long strip of cloth. **the Holy Spirit says**. This is akin to "The Lord says," common in the Old Testament prophets. **the Jews in Jerusalem will ... deliver him into Gentile hands**. While this is not strictly the way things happened (the Romans rescued Paul from the Jews who were trying to kill him), it was on account of the Jews' actions that Paul was imprisoned by the Romans.

21:27-29 Paul apparently had previous difficulties with these people (20:18-19), but now their strong nationalist and religious sentiments, heightened by the feast, were inflamed as they assumed that Paul must have brought the Gentile Trophimus into the temple. They knew Trophimus from their contacts with him at Ephesus.

23:12-13 A group of radical Jewish nationalists decided Paul must die for his supposed anti-Jewish sentiments. **bound themselves under a curse**. This was a religious commitment to kill Paul. Should they fail in the attempt, it was an acknowledgment that they themselves ought to be struck down and killed by God.

23:24 mounts. Since the plural is used, it may be that horses were provided for Paul's companions as well. **Felix the governor.** The Roman historian, Tacitus, painted a negative picture of Felix as a self-indulgent ruler who acted with disregard toward the people he was supposed to govern. He was known to have used extremely forceful measures to put down Jewish uprisings.

24:1 a lawyer. Literally, this is "an orator." Tertullus, who bears a Roman name, may have been a Greek-speaking Jew.

24:26 hoping that money would be given to him. The offering and acceptance of a bribe in such cases was illegal, but a common practice nonetheless. Paul Veyne wrote in *A History of Private Life from Pagan Rome to Byzantium*, "To our modern way of thinking, a man ceases to be a true public servant if he lines his pockets with the spoils of office or if he places personal ambition above the common good. ... The honest functionary is a peculiarity of modern Western nations. In Rome every superior stole from his subordinates. ... Every public function was a racket; those in charge 'put the squeeze' on their subordinates, and all together exploited the populace."

24:27 ***Porcius Festus***. Felix's administration ended when he was found guilty of using excessive violence in crushing a civil strife between Jews and Greeks in Caesarea. Even when forced to leave office (probably about A.D. 58), he refused to dispense with Paul's case but left him imprisoned as a favor to the Jews. He was replaced by Festus, who was governor of the area until his death 2 or 3 years later in A.D. 61.

25:9 In Jerusalem, the Sanhedrin was responsible for conducting a trial on matters of Jewish law. Festus had only to ratify a decision for capital punishment if that was what the Sanhedrin decided upon. This action was a tacit admission that Paul was innocent of violating Roman law. Since that was the only reason Paul could be held in a Roman prison, this suggestion showed that Festus was willing to sacrifice Paul for the sake of some political advantage with the Sanhedrin.

25:10-11 Paul knew there was no chance of a fair hearing in Jerusalem. Recognizing that his hope for justice lay in getting out of an area so influenced by the Sanhedrin, he exercised his right as a Roman citizen to appeal his case to the emperor.

25:13 ***King Agrippa ... in Caesarea***. The son of Herod Agrippa I (12:1), Agrippa II had been appointed as a puppet king (under Roman authority) over some provinces to the northeast of Palestine. Festus hoped he would be able to help sort out the situation with Paul because of Agrippa's Jewish background. ***Bernice***. Agrippa's sister. After her first husband died, she lived with her brother, which prompted rumors of incest. She was often presented as Agrippa's queen. She also maintained loyalty to Rome and later was the mistress of Titus, who became emperor.

To Finish Well

LAST WEEK

Last week we looked at the mixed messages Paul received as he prepared to take the offering of the Gentile churches to those in Jerusalem. On the one hand, he felt supernaturally led to go to Jerusalem one last time. On the other hand, several prophecies indicated he would suffer imprisonment and harsh treatment if he went. Paul's friends focused on the prophecies and insisted God did not want him to go. Paul balanced both messages and felt that God wanted him to go to Jerusalem in order to suffer. To apply these passages, we explored the difficult truth that walking in God's will does not guarantee us freedom from calamity and suffering.

ICEBREAKER

Most of us are better at starting things than finishing them. Who knows how many unfinished home-repair projects are represented here! One of the major tasks of Christian discipleship is learning how to persevere and finish with enthusiasm the things God gives us to do.

1. When you were a boy, which of the following was something you loved to finish?
   a. Licking the knife or spatula after Mom iced a cake
   b. Baseball season
   c. Working a jigsaw puzzle
   d. Homework
   e. Other _____

2. Who in your family (parents and siblings) was best at finishing things? Who was worst? Give examples.

3. Which of the following is something you have trouble finishing?
   a. Fixing a leaky faucet
   b. Cleaning the garage
   c. Establishing a regular family devotional time
   d. Losing that "spare tire" around my waist
   e. Other _____

Standing alongside Paul was the most dangerous place in the world to be and the safest place in the world at the same time. He seemed to be a lightning rod for opposition and disaster. Events crashed and thundered about him. Yet God's peace and protection were there too. Paul stayed true to God's purposes for his life, and God stayed true to His promises to walk with His child through everything.

Down the Home Stretch

[1] When it was decided that we were to sail to Italy, they handed over Paul and some other prisoners to a centurion named Julius, of the Imperial Regiment. [2] So when we had boarded a ship of Adramyttium, we put to sea ...

[14] But not long afterwards, a fierce wind called the "northeaster" rushed down from the island. [15] Since the ship was caught and was unable to head into the wind, we gave way to it and were driven along. ...

[23] [Paul said,] "For this night an angel of the God I belong to and serve stood by me, [24] saying, 'Don't be afraid, Paul. You must stand before Caesar. And, look! God has graciously given you all those who are sailing with you.' [25] Therefore, take courage, men, because I believe God that it will be just the way it was told to me. [26] However, we must run aground on a certain island." ...

[1] Safely ashore, we then learned that the island was called Malta. ...

[11] After three months we set sail in an Alexandrian ship that had wintered at the island, with the Twin Brothers as its figurehead. ...[14] And so we came to Rome. ...

[17] After three days he called together the leaders of the Jews. And when they had gathered he said to them: "Brothers, although I have done nothing against our people or the customs of our forefathers, I was delivered as a prisoner from Jerusalem into the hands of the Romans [18] who, after examining me, wanted to release me, since I had not committed a capital offense. [19] Because the Jews objected, I was compelled to appeal to Caesar; it was not as though I had any accusation against my nation. [20] So, for this reason I've asked to see you and speak to you. In fact, it is for the hope of Israel that I'm wearing this chain."

[21] And they said to him, "We haven't received any letters about you from Judea; none of the brothers has come and reported or spoken anything evil about you. [22] But we consider it suitable to hear from you what you think. For concerning this sect, we are aware that it is spoken against everywhere." ...

[30] Then he stayed two whole years in his own rented house. And he welcomed all who visited him, [31] proclaiming the kingdom of God and

teaching the things concerning the Lord Jesus Christ with full boldness and without hindrance.

Acts 27:1-2a,14-15,23-26; 28:1,11,14b,17-22,30-31

[6] For I am already being poured out as a drink offering, and the time for my departure is close. [7] I have fought the good fight, I have finished the race, I have kept the faith. [8] In the future, there is reserved for me the crown of righteousness, which the Lord, the righteous Judge, will give me on that day, and not only to me, but to all those who have loved His appearing.
[9] Make every effort to come to me soon, [10] for Demas has deserted me, because he loved this present world, and has gone to Thessalonica. Crescens has gone to Galatia, Titus to Dalmatia. [11] Only Luke is with me. Bring Mark with you, for he is useful to me in the ministry. ...
[16] At my first defense, no one came to my assistance, but everyone deserted me. May it not be counted against them. [17] But the Lord stood with me and strengthened me, so that the proclamation might be fully made through me, and all the Gentiles might hear. So I was rescued from the lion's mouth. [18] The Lord will rescue me from every evil work and will bring me safely into His heavenly kingdom. To Him be the glory forever and ever! Amen.

2 Timothy 4:6-11,16-18

PRINCIPLES TO LIVE BY

Paul lived his life in a focused manner. He understood the spiritual gifts God had given him. He understood his personal passion to minister the gospel where no one else had proclaimed it. He understood the call of God to be the apostle to the Gentiles. As his life drew to a close, he never took his eyes off the guiding Light that had steered him to that point. Consequently, Paul lived faithfully and productively to the very end.

PRINCIPLE 1

GOD EXPRESSES HIS PERFECT WILL IN HIS REVEALED WORD AND GIVES US A GREAT DEAL OF FREEDOM WITHIN THESE DIVINE GUIDELINES.

As his third missionary journey ended, Paul knew by revelation he should go to Jerusalem to deliver the gift from the Gentile churches and that once he arrived he would be arrested and imprisoned (Acts 19:21; 20:22-23; 21:10-13). At the same time, he hoped to stop over at Rome on the way to Spain (Rom. 15:24,28). Those were personal goals in keeping with his divine mission to take the gospel to the Gentiles, but Paul had no revelation from God mandating this mission.

The pattern of Paul's ministry seemed to be a broad brushstroke revelation from God that allowed Paul to fill in many of the details. God would intervene if He disagreed with Paul's choices. For instance, during the second missionary journey, once Paul revisited the churches established on the first trip, he began searching for the next logical field of ministry farther west or north in Asia Minor (Acts 16:6-7). The Lord, however, prevented Paul from doing what seemed obvious and used a night vision to get him to take a big leap across the Aegean Sea to Macedonia in northern Greece (vv. 8-10).

We don't know if Paul ever got to Spain. If he did, it wasn't according to his original plan. God used Paul's imprisonment in Caesarea as a time for him to testify to the secular authorities. He used Paul's right as a Roman citizen to appeal his case to the imperial court to get the Empire to pay for Paul's transportation. Paul's witness penetrated the staff and household of Nero as a result of the way God allowed events surrounding Paul's circumstances to unfold. All the while, there was a dynamic interaction between the overarching will of God and Paul's personal plans about the details of his life.

As we read the Bible, it becomes obvious very quickly that God has given us a great deal of freedom in making choices. For example, He doesn't tell us where to live, what college to enroll in, what church to attend, where to work, whom to marry, how many children to have, how much money to make, or when to retire.

However, wherever we live or attend college, we are not to participate in sinful activities that violate the will of God. Whatever church we attend, we are to fellowship with true believers and attend regularly. When we choose a business or spouse, we are not to be in relationships with nonbelievers that make it difficult, if not impossible to live fully for the Lord. When it comes to making money, God doesn't tell us "how much is enough," but He tells us always to be generous and to give to God's work regularly and proportionately. In essence, the Bible is filled with guidelines to help us make right decisions that are always in harmony with God's will.

PRINCIPLE 2

GOD WILL GIVE US DIVINE WISDOM WHEN WE ASK FOR IT. WE MUST NOT UNDERSTAND THIS WISDOM TO BE EQUAL TO OR THE SAME AS DIVINE REVELATION.

God sets out His will in the guidelines of Scripture. Then He gives us liberty to make choices in obedience to and conformity with those guidelines. He also wants to assist us in making these decisions. James wrote, "Now if any of you lacks wisdom, he should ask God, who gives to all generously and without criticizing, and it will be given to him" (Jas. 1:5).

Paul undoubtedly sought divine wisdom in planning his missionary activity to fulfill the Lord's call as apostle to the Gentiles. This did not guarantee that his plans would be infallibly aligned with the details of God's will. We should align our plans with the biblical statements about God's will. We should consult the counsel of wise believers as we make major decisions.

However, when all is said and done, we must humbly admit that our wisest decisions are not infallible in the sense that God's revealed Word is infallible. We must always say in our hearts, if not aloud, "If the Lord wills, we will live and do this or that" (4:15).

PRINCIPLE 3

GOD WANTS ALL OF US TO FINISH THE RACE—WHATEVER WE UNDERSTAND THE RACE TO BE—WITH STRENGTH AND WITH GRACE.

Paul trusted the Lord throughout the years of turmoil and uncertainty that led to his death. He often seemed the calmest person in the room (or on the ship!). He exhibited grace under pressure during his two-year imprisonment in Caesarea. He literally took charge of the ship that was carrying him in chains to Rome during the violent storm that threatened the lives of everyone on board. He acted as a soothing, healing presence amid the superstitious populace of Malta.

In Rome, Paul immediately reached out to the Jewish community in compassion and concern. As his Roman imprisonment and trial dragged on, he composed letters to the Philippian, Ephesian, and Colossian churches and to his friend, Philemon. After his release, Paul calmly resumed his travels and ministry. He penned 1 Timothy and Titus during this final interval of ministry.

After his second arrest, Paul wrote 2 Timothy from a Roman dungeon. Gone were the days of house arrest when he could receive visitors and correspond freely with the outside. Execution loomed on the horizon. Paul wrote his protégé, "I am already being poured out as a drink offering, and the time for my departure is close. I have fought the good fight, I have finished the race, I have kept the faith. In the future, there is reserved for me the crown of righteousness, which the Lord, the righteous Judge, will give me on that day" (2 Tim. 4:6-8a).

Letting up with the finish line in sight after coming so far and enduring all that he endured didn't make any sense to Paul. He finished his race with passion and grace. It is God's will that all of us achieve this same goal. The writer of Hebrews challenges us: "Therefore since we also have such a large cloud of witnesses surrounding us, let us lay aside every weight and the sin that so easily ensnares us, and run with endurance the race that lies before us, keeping our eyes on Jesus, the source and perfecter of our faith" (12:1-2a).

QUESTIONS FOR INTERACTION

1. What spiritual legacy would you like to leave your family and friends? How would you like them to remember you?

2. By what qualities would you like your old age to be characterized?

3. Why do you think God let a deadly storm assail Paul's voyage to Rome (Acts 27:14-15,23-26)? What might Paul have learned from those events?

4. How did Paul spend his first two-year imprisonment in Rome (28:17-22,30-31)?

5. Paul wrote 2 Timothy during his second Roman imprisonment, probably after a three-year span of freedom. What did Paul expect the outcome of his second trial to be (2 Tim. 4:6)?

6. What had Paul's experience been like during his second imprisonment (vv. 9-11,16)?

7. What was the state of Paul's courage and confidence (vv. 7-8,17-18)?

8. How could Paul remain so positive in such negative circumstances?

9. How do you need to live now in order to have a positive attitude about your life as you near its end?

GOING DEEPER

10. The Scripture suggests that God's will is a broad framework within which we have the responsibility of making decisions. Where do you see that your decision making ends and begins? Why?

11. Why is the subjective guidance God gives us by His Spirit and wisdom not to be put on the same level of authority as His revealed Word?

12. What are some things that can draw us away from finishing well as we grow older and near the end of life?

13. How can we minimize the impact of some of the things we mentioned in the question above?

 ## CARING TIME

As we come to the end of our study on the life of the Apostle Paul, one of the best things we can do to finish well is reflect on the principles we want to work on in the future. Too often, we complete a study and soon forget what it was about. Paul needs to be an unforgettable character, whose teachings and example continue to be a catalyst for change long into the future.

1. As you look back over this study what stands out to you as the dominant trait of Paul's character?

2. As you consider all that you have thought about during these lessons, in what major area would you like your life to become more like Paul's life?

3. Each man should summarize his answer to question 2 on a sheet of paper circulated around the group. If the group continues to meet, the leader should review this sheet with the group periodically.

SCRIPTURE NOTES

ACTS 27:1-2A,14-15,23-26; 28:1,11-31

27:1 When it was decided that we were to sail to Italy. The trip to Rome probably began sometime in the autumn of A.D. 59. ***other prisoners.*** They may also have appealed to Caesar or were to appear in the arena.

27:2 we. The "we" passages of Acts indicate that Luke was accompanying Paul at the time (16:10-17; 20:5-15; 21:1-18; 27:1–28:16).

27:14 Along the way, the wind shifted from a gentle southerly breeze to a violent northeast storm. ***a fierce wind.*** The Greek word behind this expression is the source of the English word "typhoon."

27:15 Ships of old could not face the destructive, heavy seas, so sailors had to allow the wind to push the ship away from the land.

27:23-26 In the midst of Paul's despair, God gave him a message of encouragement to pass on to the crew. While there would be the loss of the ship, all of the travelers would be spared.

28:11 *After three months we set sail in an Alexandrian ship*. Assuming that the party left Fair Havens (27:8) in mid-October, the three months at Malta would most likely include November – January, meaning they sailed again in February, still considered to be a dangerous time to be on the sea. *Twin Brothers*. Castor and Pollux, the twin sons of Zeus and Leda, were the patron saints of sailors in Greek mythology. It was customary for a ship to have their figurehead on its bow.

28:17 As soon as possible, Paul called together the leaders of the synagogues in Rome (at least 13 are known to have existed). He held this meeting in order to explain his situation to them firsthand, so they would be influenced by personal information rather than rumors.

28:19 *my nation*. Notice also "our people" and "our forefathers" (v. 17). Luke presented Christianity as established among the Jewish community in Rome for at least 20 years and perhaps as far back as Pentecost nearly 30 years earlier (2:10). Paul's letter to Rome, written some 3 years before his arrival, dealt extensively with conflicts arising between Jewish and Gentile elements in the church there. These Jewish leaders certainly knew something of Christianity, but may have desired to finally get some answers to questions that had never been clearly explained to them.

2 TIMOTHY 4:6-11,16-18

4:9 *Paul began with his main request*. He wanted Timothy to leave his post at Ephesus and join him in Rome. *come to me soon*. It would not be an easy journey nor a particularly quick one, given travel conditions in the first century. Rome was over 1,000 miles from Ephesus. Still, with the typical delays in the Roman judicial system, Paul anticipated that if Timothy hurried (and got on a boat before the shipping closed down for the winter – v. 21), there would be adequate time for him to reach Rome before his trial.

4:10-11 Next, Paul explained the reason why he wanted Timothy to come. It seemed that all his colleagues had left him (with the exception of Luke), either by reason of defection (Demas) or because of ministry needs (Crescens and Titus). *Bring Mark with you*. It is a remarkable testimony to the power of the Holy Spirit that after the argument over Mark, which had resulted in the split between Paul and Barnabas (because Mark had deserted them in Perga on their very first missionary journey – Acts 13:13; 15:36-41), reconciliation had taken place. Mark was once again a valued co-worker with Paul (v. 24; Col. 4:10; Philem. 24).

NOTES

NOTES

NOTES